Jeff Slapdash has been a bodger since birth. He took up journalism at the tender age of 21, and has since been thrown off the editorial staff of every DIY magazine you care to name.

Undaunted, he is still in regular contact with fellow dedicated bodgers, and up-to-date with all the latest bodging techniques and skills.

Though Jeff has written many books on bodging, this is the first to find a publisher brave enough to print it. And so, this is his first major opportunity to reach out to all the closet bodgers in the world, hungry for his wealth of knowledge and experience.

Jeff lives with his wife and ten children (he made quite a bodge-up of the family planning, too) in a rundown, dilapidated, one-year-old house somewhere in North London. All the neighbours have moved away.

The Sporting Life

BODGE IT YOURSELF

A beginner's guide to B I Y

JEFF SLAPDASH

ILLUSTRATED BY
ODETTE BUCHANAN

ARROW BOOKS

Arrow Books Limited
62–65 Chandos Place, London WC2N 4NW

An imprint of Century Hutchinson Limited

London Melbourne Sydney Auckland
Johannesburg and agencies throughout
the world

First published in Great Britain 1986

Photoset in Linotron Plantin by
Rowland Phototypesetting Limited
Bury St Edmunds, Suffolk
Printed and bound in Great Britain by
Blantyre Printing & Binding Limited
London and Glasgow

ISBN 0 09 940470 2

CONTENTS

To Chris

This book is respectfully dedicated to a small band of unsung heroes.

Men and women who have given themselves unselfishly to their art, often at great risk to life and limb (although rarely their own), and who openly defy one of the most humdrum conventions of our present-day society.

Who are these courageous few, this breed apart, you may ask, and what is it that unites them in their common cause?

Supporters of the Geoffrey Boycott for England campaign? Surely not.

Well, some Terry Wogan fans then? Hardly.

Or perhaps some misguided SDP–Liberal Alliance candidates standing for some obscure northern by-elections?

No, friends, the answer is that these wonderful people are quite simply experts in the noblest of arts: *Bodge It Yourself*. They are *Bodgers*.

Not for them the boring restrictions of Do It Yourself. These brave men and women have made the daunting decision to ignore the call of *Practical Householder*.

To them, track lighting is still something that Daley Thompson trains under.

And the mention of a 'tip from the trade' conjures up a suggestion from the local bookmaker.

These are the people who haven't got the knack, and have no desire to get it.

These are the people who proudly refuse to accept the sheer joy of bidet installation, and who stand their ground when it comes to investing their hard-earned weekend insulating the loft.

Unlike their DIY counterparts, *bodgers* have no interest in boring the unsuspecting with details of their exploits – and have, for the most part, denied their ability in order to protect their sacred art. For, to the bodger, BIY is a form of expression as important to man's appreciation of the finer things in life as the Cubism movement was to painting.

Today, however, after years of living in the shadow of DIYers, with rawlplugs in their pockets and a year's supply of sandpaper in the kitchen drawer, the tide is unquestionably turning in favour of BIY. As the movement goes from strength to strength, we will all soon be able to chuckle openly at the DIYer's onyx matching taps, giggle at his suspended ceiling and guffaw at his cork tiling. No longer will we have to be intimidated by the pictures in *Homes and Gardens*. No longer will the lone bodger think that only he has to be coerced into building kitchen cabinets. That only he finds no satisfaction in a hard day at the workmate.

Yes, friends, the bodging movement is taking off – and not a moment too soon if you ask me.

DIY has been seeping into the very pores of society for too long now, and must be restricted at every corner. There is hardly any place left to avoid the cursed DIYers with their graph paper and expert advice. Be honest. How many dinner parties have you attended where you've been placed next to some chap extolling the virtues and explaining the gruesome details of his loft conversion? How many times have you been caught in a golfing foursome with a chap who was building his own patio and barbecue area, and saw no reason why you shouldn't hear about the laying of every brick?

The time has come for bodgers to put their collective foot down (but mind where you're treading). Black & Decker and the like threaten the very fibre of our nation.

Could this be the year that you come out of the closet and join the cause (providing, of course, that you haven't already bodged the lock, in which case you'll need some help from outside)? The year that you throw away your sander and drill and take up darts?

Let me, Jeff Slapdash, as your mentor and guide, steer you off the straight and narrow of DIY and through the tricky winding path of BIY.

Don't hide your true feelings behind a thin veil of DIY respectability. Yours could be the greatest bodging talent of them all.

For bodgers throughout the land agree the time has come to make a stand.

This is not the beginning of the end, just the end of the beginning.

It's all there, just outside your reach.

So go for it. You're bound to miss.

Good luck and good bodging. And remember the bodger's motto . . .

IF A JOB'S WORTH BODGING
IT'S WORTH BODGING WELL

HAVE YOU GOT WHAT IT TAKES?

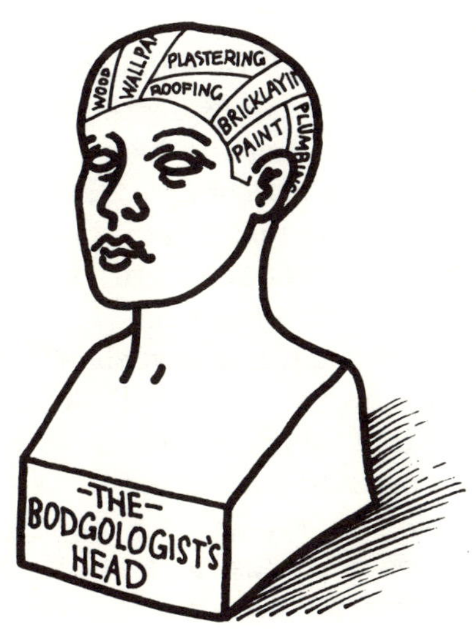

To be a bodger demands the right mental attitude.

DIYers might argue rather gauchely that being mental alone helps, but this, of course, is petty jealousy.

So what is a bodger, and, more importantly, what makes him tick?

Put simply, the bodger is to home improvements what Robert Carrier is to car mechanics.

A bodger is the sort of ordinary Joe who throws away the instruction manual when he opens the box, and thinks the printed legend on the side of the box which reads 'Open Other End' only applies to other people.

He's the sort of chap who never starts anything he might finish, and never finishes anything he might start. He is not (as some) obsessed with completion, being quite capable of flitting from the sitting room to the bathroom, to the front garden, to the back room, from the hallway to the bedroom and back to the sitting room, leaving a trail of unfinished shelves, half-painted walls, unsecured light fittings and missing floorboards for a despairing family to discover at their peril. His is not the fussy, small-minded character of the compulsive DIYer. He doesn't become restless if the shelves of the bookcase aren't quite parallel. He knows that there is more to life than toggle bolts. He understands that happiness is not necessarily dependent on having handles on every door or windows that actually open.

Even in his youth, our friend would have shown something of the stuff he was made of. Having ignored the instructions with his Airfix kit, he was the only kid in his street with a propellerless, pilotless and undercarriageless Spitfire.

The only boy in his class who never made his own toolbox. This is not to imply, however, that our man is in any way lazy. Au contraire, he deliberately rushes the mundane jobs or avoids them as the case may be, so that he can indulge in more rewarding pursuits. Who wants to watch the paint dry in the kitchen when he could be watching the ball soar over the fairway? Who wants to spend a Saturday papering the bathroom when he could be cheering the local team on to victory? Is wood panelling more important than fishing? Indirect lighting more life-enhancing than a good game of squash?

And, of course, the bodger needs time to pursue more cerebral activities such as his study of architecture (we refer you to the *Frank Lloyd Wright Good Pub Guide*).

So, how does one become a bodger? Well, that's almost like asking how one becomes a saint. As yet, there are no application forms, direct lines or evening classes.

Which is why I have devised a little aptitude test to sort out the men from the boys, the plodders from the daredevils, the BIYers from the DIYers.

Its purpose is to establish your credentials to bodge.

Get a pencil and have a go.

	YES	NO
1. Are you the sort of person who puts tools away after every job?	☐	☐
2. Do you sweep up after drilling a hole in the skirting board?	☐	☐
3. Do you deny that a six-inch nail is your favourite solution to any problem?	☐	☐
4. Do you separate your wood screws from the rest?	☐	☐
5. Do you prefer drilling and rawl-plugging to using a masonry nail?	☐	☐
6. Do you and your wife wear matching sweaters?	☐	☐

7. Would you always rub down the undercoat before putting on another layer of paint? ☐ ☐

8. Do you always check before putting a nail in a floorboard to see if a pipe is running beneath it? ☐ ☐

9. Do you paint underneath shelves as well? ☐ ☐

10. Do your overalls bear a designer name? ☐ ☐

11. Do you subscribe to a monthly magazine that slowly builds up into an encyclopaedia of DIY knowledge? ☐ ☐

12. Would you use three grades of sandpaper for one job? ☐ ☐

13. Do you always read the instructions from a DIY book stage by stage as you do the job? ☐ ☐

14. Do you invite people around to talk about the improvements you've made? ☐ ☐

15. Do you measure up wood with a T square? ☐ ☐

16. Do you use a countersink drill?

17. Do you stir paint for the required time – or even longer?

18. Do you possess a plumb line?

19. Do you visit DIY megastores and just browse around, usually buying something that will come in useful one day?

20. Does your lawn look like Wembley on a Saturday afternoon in May?

21. Do you get the wife to save empty marmalade jars for your screws and things?

22. Do you drive a Volvo?

23. Do you cover furniture with sheets before painting the ceiling?

24. Have you ever sought professional advice on decorating matters?

25. Do you watch *Gardener's World*?

26. Have you ever attended evening classes for woodwork?

27. Do you know the difference between a compression and a capillary joint? ☐ ☐

28. Do you wrap your chisels in oily cloths and store them in a dry place? ☐ ☐

29. Do you own *two* extension cables? ☐ ☐

30. Do you fill in aptitude tests in books and magazines? ☐ ☐

Well, how did you do?

If you got one or two yesses amongst the nos you're possible bodger material.

However, too many yesses suggests that you are beyond help. See a doctor soon.

Those who passed with a majority of nos have a natural talent and can now read on and be proud to bodge.

Don't hide your light under a bushel (you'll probably only succeed in setting fire to it).

If you really want to bodge, and you've got it in you, then this book will bring it out.

Always assuming, of course, that it doesn't fall apart before you've finished it.

Too err is human, to bodge divine

INTERIOR DECORATING

To the experienced bodger interior decorating offers no real problems at all. Procrastination will keep you safe for a time at least. And in this you can rely on the unwitting help of the good wife as she lends a hand to the rope that hoists her own petard. Because of her own concern over the selection of paints, materials and wallpaper patterns, this is one instance when she is the answer to a bodger's prayers.

Remember, also, that subtle remarks about the vagaries of fashion, doubts about the compatibility of certain totally suitable colours and patterns, and suggestions that 'her at number 47' did a similar thing last year will have the poor woman umming and arring for months. A regular order of magazines such as *Interiors, Ideal Home, House and Garden* etc. will also help to fan the fires of indecision, thus buying you more and more time.

With so much to read and so little to decorate, the trouble and strife should be so confused she'll shelve the whole project until the headaches have gone away.

As every good bodger knows, however, all good things must come to an end, eventually. You must, therefore, be prepared for the dreaded day when the light of your life decides on the design she wants, and nothing short of a tornado will get you another reprieve.

This section is split into two areas of interior decorating: wallpapering and painting. Under each heading you'll find useful tips on how to do the quickest and least bothersome job – and how to discourage any similar projects for many months (or years, if you're really good) to come.

PAINTING

Painting offers the least expensive and easiest way of changing and brightening the appearance of one's home. Once you accept this dreadful fact, the true bodger can set about dealing with this most recurrent form of home decoration.

It is therefore imperative that you learn how to avoid painting tasks when and wherever they occur, if not before. A good bodger will always think ahead, being able to sense danger and impending doom months in advance by recognising the early clues. Such phrases as 'I can never get the sitting room really clean these days' or 'I've spent all day giving our bedroom a good old fashioned top-to-bottom but it still looks like it did yesterday' should not be lightly dismissed. Staying alert for such phrases as these is of the utmost importance if you are going to be able to accurately sense the mood of the opposition – and attempt to deflect it.

These oblique remarks will undoubtedly continue to mount up in the days, weeks and months ahead; until that fateful day when you realise with one throwaway sentence from your true love that the moment of action cannot be so very far away: 'I'm going to give the front room furniture a move around this afternoon . . . see if that'll help . . . Maureen's coming around to give me a hand'. That's it. Red alert. All hands to the beer pumps. You've just had the jolly old warning shot across the bows.

No, she isn't going to transform the front room into a passable imitation of a British Rail waiting room. The interjection of another female name, be it Maureen, Connie, Angela, Sandra or Patricia, spells danger with a capital D. The next step will be that when you return home after a hard day at the office, wanting nothing more than a little peace and quiet and a chance to relax, the wall-to-wall shag pile will be covered with wall-to-wall magazine articles and paint cards. There'll be the usual mindblowing marigolds, revolting rustic pinks, sickening sunset oranges and swamp greens. As the dearly beloved caresses your worried brow and fetches your slippers you'll quickly realise that this isn't Wednesday night again. Yes, dear apprentice bodger, as your wife points out the subtle difference between Honeysuckle and Magnolia (as interesting as an empty six-pack of lager), you will be able to see more than the writing on the wall.

At this point in the proceedings it's worth deciding whether you are going to be a man or a mouse. Or, to put it another way, a spineless DIYer, or a creative bodger.

Let's consider the DIYer's reaction

The DIYer, all muscle and ballcock, will launch himself into a ten-minute display of reluctance in the finest tradition of the Hollywood greats. All the eloquence of a Sylvester Stallone, all the warmth of a Clint Eastwood, all the art of gentle persuasion of a Marlon Brando and all the humour of a Charles Bronson will be brought into play.

But it is only for show. As surely as Tea Rose complements Hazelnut Matt, the wife, countering with several cups of tea, his favourite Mr Kipling Bakewell Tarts and his prewarmed slippers, would finish with her Joan Collins sashay.

And as sure as Bob's your uncle the battle is over before it's begun and within forty-eight hours Marlon's up to his eyes in rollers and masking tape and the job's done.

Life can be hard but swift on the DIY front.

Now let's consider the way the inexperienced bodger will tackle the same problem

He will start by going into frenzied inactivity, dropping his shoulders, complaining about the price of paint before retiring to the Dog and Trumpet for a few pints of Depression bitter. He will sulk. He may even threaten the summer holiday.

This will probably gain him a couple of weeks' grace, but they will be weeks of troubled grace, and in the end he will have to give in.

Now let's observe the true bodger at work

With years of cunning under his belt, the true bodger reacts as you'd expect, with complete confidence. Without batting so much as an eyelid he will appear to be putty in the rubber-gloved hands of her indoors.

That evening our experienced bodger will actually sit down and chat encouragingly to the light of his life about the project that is taking over her every waking hour. 'Is the Fuchsia range actually going to set the right mood in the sitting room, petal?' he'll ask kindly. 'How are we going to do the feature wall, my little comfort and joy?' he'll enquire with enthusiasm. 'Will it match the curtains, my delightful decorator?'

With sincerity, he will say, 'Would you prefer wall lamps or track lights, precious?' Without a smirk he will suggest, 'Shall we leave the tropical fish tank where it is, my dearest darling?' Or, 'Where will we put the collection of glass clowns your mother gave us, my angel? Should they match the curtains too?'

These are all basic questions bodgers have used over the years to keep the conversation going and the work at a standstill. Catching her off guard, they divert her attention while not committing you to anything. Try a few yourself and you'll find your wife and friends amazed at how well you seem to be taking it all.

Or so they think.

Having swum with the tide, as it were, it's the following day that the real bodger will set about putting the project on the rocks.

Enthusiasm, that's the tactic of the bodger. He'll bring home a plethora of magazines for the good lady to peruse, together with colour swatches of paint and wallpaper samples. Examples of fuchsia pinks and starburst yellows by the truckload. Handled correctly, enough confusion can be generated by this extreme amount of choice – and a state of semi-permanent indecision induced by the simple repetition of the question, 'But what about the . . .' – to banish all thoughts of repainting the front room until sanity returns. Which should take months at least. In fact, by the time she is ready to tackle the subject again it will be something else's turn for attention – and another opportunity to stall for one more season.

This is all very well, but it must be remembered that such success will only be available to the experienced bodger. For the rest of you the 'front room' project will remain on the cards despite your most excellent efforts. If, in spite of everything, you come home one night to find drip cloths on the carpet and sheets over the furniture, you still have one more card up your sleeve. Take the wife for a little drive to the nearest giant DIY store. Keen with enthusiasm, parade her past the new kitchens, the gardening section, and the lighting displays, and slowly lead her up to the 'Mixmaster' paint machine. A fiendishly clever device, the 'Mixmaster' actually mixes the exact paint colour you want right there before your very eyes. Here she will be subjected to a choice of at least 128 shades of yellow, 234 shades of red, 168 shades of green and so on, enough to make even the Dulux dog go weak. In fact, Mixmasters with their mindboggling varieties have turned many an uncertain customer several shades of green and have been known to put off even avid DIYers.

If the wife can survive this ordeal she deserves to have the front room painted.

Equipment – the right tools for the best job

DIY books always stress that with the right equipment decorating takes less time and effort and good results are guaranteed. Rubbish. It's like spending six hours preparing a gourmet meal when all you wanted in the first place was a hamburger. If you take ages hunting around for plumb lines and stripping knives, sponges and buckets and glass-paper blocks, step-ladders, paint kettles, blowlamps and brushes, you'll be so exhausted by the end of it that you won't have the strength to paint. Painting is boring enough without turning it into your life's avocation. All the average citizen needs to paint the average room is some paint, a couple of rags, and, of course, something with which to paint.

Paint brushes

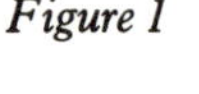

Figure 1

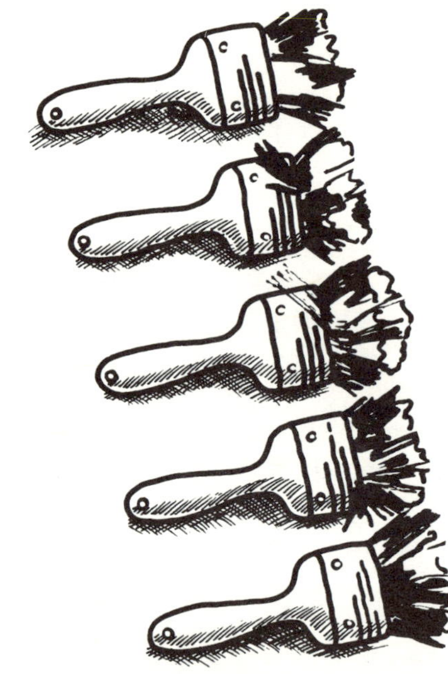

You've cottoned on, haven't you? Changing brushes every three minutes is also not only expensive, but an appalling waste of time. The true bodger quickly realises the benefits of having just one brush for all his painting needs. No more costly outlay on a dozen brushes, most of which will only see a passing glimpse of a paint pot. No more gallons of expensive brush cleaner. No more hours spent dutifully cleaning brushes which are going to wind up stiff as iron sheeting no matter how fastidious you are.

The other good thing about having only one brush is, of course, that if anyone borrows it (assuming that there is something special about this brush that stops it from being thrown out after it is used) you can't be called on to do so much as a touch-up.

The final point to remember concerning brushes is that, no matter what the local handyman tries to tell you, no paint brush ever comes really clean. Despite the bravest efforts, after one or two outings the only things it is good for is a weapon. It is, therefore, a squandering of money better spent on a new golf ball, a bottle of wine, or a good book to invest in expensive brushes. It doesn't take that much to pick out the odd hair from the paint on the wall.

Care and cleaning

As I've already hinted, you may cheerfully ignore any manufacturer's instructions about care and cleaning. To put it succinctly: What's the point? No sooner have you dissolved every little bit of congealed paint from the bristles than you're coerced into getting paint on them all over again. Even if you do get involved in the white spirit trap, we all know that at the end of the day you wind up with a brush bent stiffly into the shape of the bottom of a Nescafé jar.

As far as care goes, one place of storage is as good as another. I myself like to stash my brushes in the wife's favourite vase. When she's got something she wants painted it's the last place she looks for the brush, and it also gives me a small but invigorating sense of retaliation. DIYers don't, of course, indulge in such petty emotions, but the rest of us do.

Figure 2

Rollers

No, not the sort of rollers you find parked in Mayfair or the rollers her indoors likes to wear in bed. I refer, of course, to paint rollers, one of the few DIY tools of which the bodger can wholeheartedly approve. They are quick, easy to use and can make a two-day job into a twenty-minute jamboree. In fact, you'd think they were completely bodgeproof.

We should cocoa.

Lull your friends and loved ones into a false sense of security by convincing them that you have embraced DIY respectability with your little roller. Trick them into thinking that your days of baulking at the sight of a tin of paint are over. Demonstrate to your dinner party guests with a few dry runs of your roller across the table just how you intend tackling the job before you – and with how much *joie de vivre*.

When it actually comes to getting your roller wet, go into a devastating display of the ease and simplicity of window frame painting with a roller, or the efficiency of a roller when it comes to the ceiling (by ensuring that you only give it one thin coat, you can leave a trail of lines more complex than the siding plan for British Rail at Swindon). That should be enough to guarantee that you will never be expected to paint the wainscoting again.

Preparing the wall

It has been stated many times by members of the DIY fraternity and their minions that in order to get the correct finish and ensure against damage such as cracking, crazing or bubbling, one has to invest time and trouble in preparation. In cleaning, sanding, and priming. Balderdash. The main purpose of paint is to cover the surface. If you're not slapping on two coats of Woolworth's finest in order to cover those handprints, nail holes and spaghetti sauce stains, why are you slapping them on? And if that's the case, why waste valuable daylight hours and put your back at risk to make the wall look better than it did when the house was new, and then cover it all up with a coat of Wood Sage and Weeping Willow that would have impressed everyone enough on its own? If life is too short for the stuffing of mushrooms, it is much too short for the scraping off of any loose or flaking paint. She'll have you painting it all over again in three years anyway.

Should you come upon any of the common paint job flaws – blisters and bubbles, cracks, crazing, chips and dents, efflorescence, flaking, or mould – the best thing to do is to ignore it. Put a lot of paint on the brush and paint on. Should any of these problems erupt in a newly painted surface there are DIY things one can do to cure them, but as they all cost time and often money the simplest solution is to blame the central heating and promise to rectify them next time you paint.

Modern trends, after all, prefer the 'au naturel' look in any event – and the occasional 'mottled' effect has recently become extremely popular. So there is no need to waste time stripping old wallpaper, scraping old paint, filling in and rubbing down, because you're only going to spend time covering it all up again (see wallpapering).

Figure 3

Don't be halted by flaky walls; paint on

One coat of emulsion can cover and enhance years of old wallpaper

Cracked plaster presents no problem to the serious bodging painter

Let's paint

Despite every effort, eventually you'll get around to the actual application of the wet stuff. When you've made it this far after months and months of trying to put it off, it seems a shame not to enjoy the moment to the full.

Figure 4

Even if you weren't born with a silver spoon in your mouth, use one to open your paint tins

Look upon the painting of a room as an opportunity, even a challenge. Accept with open arms the responsibility, and amaze everyone with the verve with which you tackle the project. Let your creativity flow. Remember, for as long as you are up to your neck in paint trays and drip cloths no one is going to come up with anything else for you to do.

All DIY manuals show someone painting in an empty room. This is cheating. After all, how many people do you know who have empty rooms? Clearing a room of all its contents is hard, time-consuming, back-breaking work. Furthermore, once the room is empty there are always at least three further projects which become immediately apparent and have to be seen to before anything else can be done. Unless you want to miss every major televised sports event for the next six months it seems simply foolish to move the rug (reminding you of the condition of the floor, which will then remind her of your promise to put cork tiles in the kitchen) in the first place. So don't do it. With just a few weeks' worth of the Sunday papers, judiciously placed to keep the semi-gloss off the coffee table, you can paint around anything. And avoid the tedium of having to put everything back again anyway.

Unless you are out to beat the record for the longest time spent painting one medium sized room (three adult men, two weeks, and the window frame was never completed), I recommend tackling the job of painting at high speed. It'll all look different when it dries in any event. If a little paint should stray from the target areas you can always blame it on something else (the fly you were trying to

Figure 5 *Paint round wall cupboards, pictures, ethnic wall hangings etc.*

keep out of the paint pot). The sooner you're done, the sooner you can be doing something else.

Not only, of course, do you not have to remove furniture or carpets, you don't have to remove shelves, or pictures, flying ducks, or commemorative plates either. Who will ever know? Do you seriously think that anybody's going to remove the collected works of Jeffrey Archer from your shelves to see if the wall behind them is mauve instead of apple green? When you walk out of the room, do you think your guests immediately start peeking behind the paintings to see what the original wallpaper was? Of course not. If they did the painter's job would be a lot harder.

Figure 6

Don't remove ornaments; paint round them

Don't remove anything removable

When painting a skirting, never lift the carpet or use a paint shield

You will also find that most fixtures (such as light switches and outlets) look better when painted the same colour as the walls.

When you've finished and the brush finally plops from your weary hand the whole room should be covered in speckles of paint the same colour as the ceiling and walls. This will give a modern, totally co-ordinated look to the room (which the people next door will immediately want to imitate), and also save you the expense of buying new lamp shades and curtains to match the colour scheme.

With this bravado display you should have deterred the wife from asking you to paint another single thing for at least five years.

Mission accomplished.

How to paint a floor

Few people would admit it, but most of us, at one time or another, have looked up suddenly to find that we have painted ourselves into a corner – just like in the cartoons. Years of doing odd jobs around the house have convinced me that it is easier and far less straining to paint yourself into a corner than to not paint yourself into a corner. Follow my instructions as set out in Figure 7 and you will not only make a lasting impression but will get out of putting the cork tiles down in the kitchen once and for all.

Figure 7

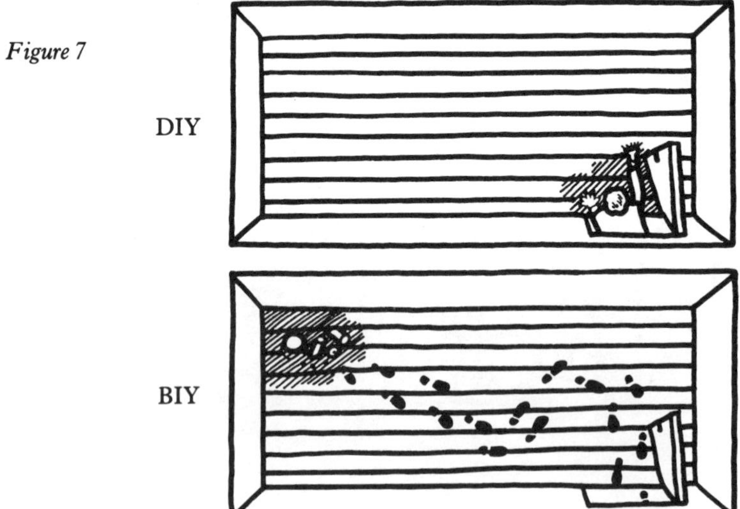

How to paint a ceiling

Step-ladders (unless you can borrow one or two) are expensive and can be dangerous. For reaching the tops of most walls, standing on a coffee table or the arm of a chair on tiptoe will do the trick, but ceilings are harder. If you are standing on something you have to keep getting down and lugging it around the room. The figure below illustrates the special roller adaptor which I have invented to make painting the ceiling the work of but a moment (I have been known to paint the entire living room ceiling just in the intermission times on a Saturday afternoon). No fuss, no bother, no vertigo – just a perfect job, quickly done.

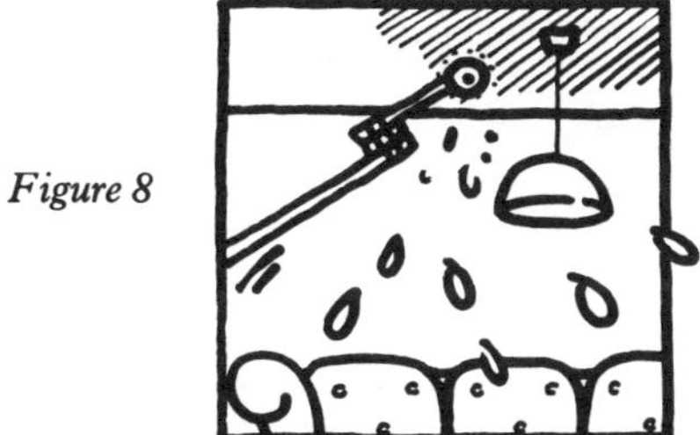

Figure 8

The fiddly bits

I've pretty much covered the larger and more easily mastered expanses of interior painting, so now we can turn our attention to what DIYers (with the patience of sheep) resign themselves to, and BIYers actively hate.

It is easy enough to ignore instructions about first rubbing down, putting on the undercoat, rubbing down, putting on the undercoat, rubbing down, putting on the top coat, rubbing down and putting on the top coat again (hard enough work to read let alone actually doing it). But the fiddly bits are where bodging comes into its own.

DIY books are all very strict when it comes to the painting of doors and windows, insisting that they must be painted in a rigid sequence. The bodger, however, uninhibited by fears of bittiness, curtains, sags or runs, can turn the painting of a window frame into a mere ten-minute job and be out in the back on a lawn chair catching up on his Russian literature while the DIYer is still waiting for the first coat to dry. As far as the true bodger is concerned, stages are something you find in theatres.

Painting a window frame

Figure 9

DIY BIY

You can waste a lot of time trying to figure out how the window was constructed so you know in what order to paint it, or fretting about investing in an aluminium shield. Give a bodger his trusty brush and a can of lager and watch him polish off a delicately-carved Victorian door in a week (or a day if there's a good movie on the box). I have known bodgers with their creative powers in full flow cover an entire Robert Adam staircase in Chinese Red gloss in no longer than it takes to run a single episode of *Crossroads*.

The sash window allows for another fine example of the serious bodger at work. The DIYer will start by taking hours to prepare, prime and apply putty, before even a drop of gloss has been applied. He'll then work out the correct order in which to paint the frame, inside and out.

The bodger, however, ignoring all this rigmarole, goes straight for the jugular, applying one and only one coat in the fastest possible time.

If this should mean that the two sashes are well and truly stuck together when the paint dries, a hefty wallop will open the window and a strategically placed plant or two will cover any chip marks where the paint has come off in the process.

How to paint a door

The door on the left shows you how a DIYer would tackle this painting job. The numbers, of course, refer to the painting sequence, something they believe in as strongly as they do completing the task in one arduous session. It is all very orderly, just like a DIYer's sock drawer.

A look at the door on the right, however, shows you a much more interesting technique, and one which the average person (who has more to do with his time than laying on, brushing in, and laying off) can readily appreciate.

The purist bodger, of course, would say that the use of months would have much more aesthetic appeal.

Figure 10

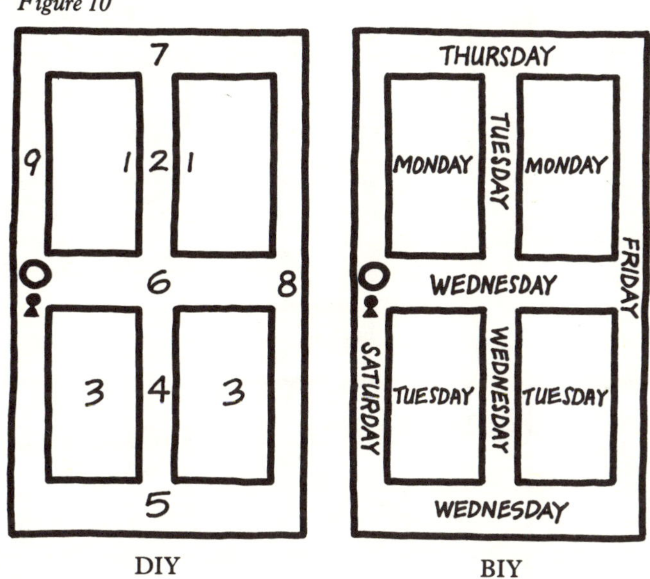

DIY BIY

Special effects

Many old and fascinating techniques in special effect painting are now freely available to the DIY fraternity: rag rolling, sponging, marbling etc. With much excitement, at least half the country has frantically thrown itself into learning these new-found practices.

A BIY man takes a much calmer view of the whole affair.

After all, everything he does with a paintbrush can be said to be a special effect. And, through the centuries, bodging father has passed on to bodging son and bodging friend has revealed to bodging friend the special tricks of the trade.

I illustrate a few here, for the curious and especially daring. Once you've mastered the basic effects, why not have a go at creating a new look all of your own? Go on, be a devil.

Figure 11

The Mousetrap effect (the showstopper that will run and run)

The Max Bygraves effect (you need hands)

The True Grit effect (paint the door or window on a windy day and leave it open)

The Short and Curlies effect (always grabs attention when discreetly placed in the middle of a door panel)

The Vinyl Flytrap effect (see how many creepy crawlies you can catch on a door panel, once again proving there are no flies on a bodger)

The Tramlines effect (an often used effect. Unlike the buses, you can be sure there'll always be another one along in a minute)

The 'Stucko' effect (put the ornaments back on the shelf before the paint dries)

The Mastermind effect (once you've started, you'll pass on one or two bits)

WALLPAPERING

The art of hanging wallpaper is not all that dissimilar from that of painting. In other words, you start off by learning how to avoid it.

In the case of wallpapering, avoidance tactics should be taken a little more seriously, as there are fewer short cuts available and it generally involves a lot more work and expense.

In your favour, of course, is the fact that the selection of the proper wallpaper is a far more complicated and time-consuming project than the selection of paint. There's only so much they can do to green, for instance. Not even the most practised bodger can haggle for more than a week and a half over the exact shade of beige for the hall. Wallpaper, however, is a field with real scope.

Begin with the sample books. As the poor woman paws over the mountains of paper in different colours, patterns, weights and textures, keep making suggestions. 'But what about that tartan, love?' 'I thought you loved those raised peacocks Aunt Katie had in her lounge.' 'Didn't you say that imitation leather would look good in the study?'

When you've finally agreed, throw in another thought and start all over again. Seek out every wallpaper shop you can find in your area, and then move further afield. Every time she thinks she's found the paper of her dreams, remember a similar but better pattern you saw somewhere else. If she queries the reason why she's looking at the paper sample book for Campbells of Dumfries when you live in Surbiton, point out that their patterns are infinitely better than, say, those of Hughes of Swansea, Harrison of Morecambe, or Bass of Bournemouth.

That night in bed when she repels your amorous advances with 'I've got a headache', you'll know it's the genuine article and you will be able to shut your eyes and rejoin Alan Lamb on the pitch at Old Trafford in your record-breaking partnership against the West Indies.

This tactic will gain you a few weeks' grace. W.G. style.

Preparation

Sooner, although I hope it will be later, than you think you'll have to do some wallpapering. Life is like that.

All the manuals written for avid DIYers stress the need for surface preparation beforehand. My rule on this particular phase of the exercise is once again simplicity itself. Don't.

No self-respecting bodger would waste valuable time washing down walls or scraping flaky paint from the plaster. Nor would he treat the walls with size to seal the surface. Applying the thinnest lining paper to an uneven surface is also unheard of in bodging circles. Who really cares? Do you really want to spend sixteen hours of your life on a task that only Harry from next door will ever notice? Of course you don't.

Another DIY practice, that of making good cracks in plaster, also seems pretty pointless to a real bodger. So don't bother. By the same token, you should never strip old wallpaper. There is a very good reason for this, and one that DIYers would be wise to consider. A general build-up of wallpaper over the years not only provides insulation and soundproofing for free, but also makes the area that needs wallpapering progressively smaller each year. Thus saving the cost of expensive insulation and double glazing.

Bodgers do it in the next six months

Equipment

Always have everything you need ready before you start

So what are the tools you need to easily, quickly and successfully wallpaper?

Well, first you need a pasting table. Almost any handy table will do, though, ideally, it should be slightly narrower than the roll of paper you are endeavouring to paste. Any available knife or pair of scissors will do (though the wife's manicuring scissors do have a tendency to leave scalloped edges or veer off in strange directions). You will also need a paste brush to slop the paste on to the paper, and a sponge to mop up any excess (there is no need to go out and buy a sponge especially for this job – just make sure that you don't take one that has seen too much service in the bathroom bowl, and wives do have a tendency to get excited if you grab the natural sponge they use for their ablutions).

A plastic bucket is also essential equipment as it will hold the paste, and later provide a handy receptacle for empty beer cans (at a pinch, though, a large wastepaper basket or plant holder can be substituted for your actual plastic pail). And, of course, you'll need the wallpaper paste itself. If you haven't any left from your last redecorating escapade in '67, go out and buy the cheapest brand you can find (so at least if for any strange reason you someday find yourself having to take the stuff off again it will come away easily). There is no need to worry about things like plumb lines or angle rollers. As in any other such project, exactitude is a time-consuming and unnecessary expenditure of energy.

Your equipment assembled, you need only add those implements necessary to any reasonable man's well-being to complete the picture: a radio (or, better still, a portable TV), a newspaper for when you get bored, and a supply of liquid refreshment. A few rolls of wallpaper is then all that is needed for the work to commence.

Wall to wall paper

Whether the final choice be Regency stripe, vinyl, chip paper, heavy duty, hessian, simulated grass, flock, waterproof, mirrorfinish, matt, patterned or plain really doesn't matter to the bodger because every roll receives the same considered attention.

It is a simple fact, however, that the thicker the paper the more it covers in terms of previous indiscretions. Thus a drop of damp can easily be coped with by using a roll or two of Anaglypta. A touch of dry rot is child's play with a coating of Vymura Heavy. And fungus is a mere bagatelle to Hessian. If the worst comes to the worst and nothing will cover your particular problem follow the ancient bodging answer to troublesome walls and hoist up a rug or two.

When it comes to measuring and calculating the number of rolls you'll need there's no point in resorting to anything so sordid or degrading as mathematics, geometry or nuclear physics. The bodger's rule of thumb is to take your age next birthday, add fifteen, multiply by three and divide by six. This will provide you with either enough paper (depending on your age) to re-paper the whole of your street, or, conversely, enough to cover two-thirds of a very small boxroom.

Figure 13

DIY

BIY

The latter is always preferable. It should also be pointed out that if the paper chosen is the last of a discontinued line or only available in a slightly different colour you will be able to buy it cheap.

Having purchased the required design in an unknown quantity, and having dismissed any attempt to prepare the walls, bodging can begin in earnest.

Mixing the paste is easy as no stirring is required. The solution, when ready to paste, should fall into the lumpy custard category or be watery enough to have the adhesive power of a soluble aspirin. The benefit of either is that even hours after you've pasted the paper to the wall you can always change your mind and take it down again intact.

All wallpaper lengths should be measured with the aid of your eye only. Err on the side of too long as opposed to a short length, and just a quick snip with the scissors will save you from all that laborious measuring and marking that goes on in the DIY semi.

Once pasted, proceed to the wall as shown in Figure 13.

Going to the wall

DIYers, who like to give themselves a sense of self-importance, will tell you that this is a complicated and difficult job, but in truth nothing is simpler than attaching a length of paper to a wall. The consistency of your paste does, of course, affect the ease of this operation. The thicker the paste, the more attracted the paper is to the wall. On the other hand, the thinner it is the easier it is to manoeuvre with it (or, if the worst comes to the worst, remove it). If you get into any real trouble, you can, of course, resort to either a large roll of double-sided tape or a six-inch nail.

Figure 14

The correct wallpaper paste consistency is very important for a proper job

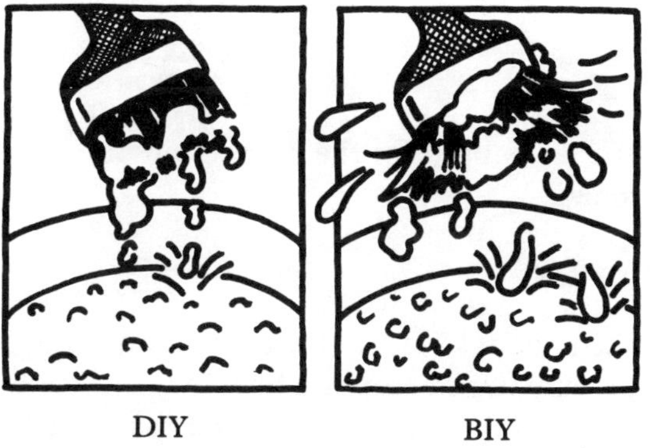

DIY BIY

Forget anything you might have heard in passing about matching, aligning, establishing a true vertical measure, hanging, trimming, or turning corners. Put the paste on the paper; put the paper on the wall. If the paper should accidentally tear while you're trying to straighten it out or get the roses near one another, you will probably be able to put a duck or something over it later so that no one will ever notice. Or blame it on dampness.

At the end of the day, when the job is more or less done, you may find you have one or two problems to explain. If there is a 4mm gap between sheets, the line to take is that you have done this on purpose to allow for what we in the trade call paper-stretch. If after a day, however, you find yourself with a 8mm gap between sheets due to paper shrinkage, you should explain that these are 'condensation runways', specially designed to allow any condensation to run away.

Papering ceilings

A word about papering ceilings. Don't.

Brinkmanship, bodger style

The name of the game is to see just how far you can go before the wife notices that something is drastically wrong.

Here are three tests of her IQ (Irritation Quota).

1. Make no attempt whatsoever to match the repeat pattern. *(Score five points)*
2. Put the paper on upside down. *(Score ten points)*
3. Put the wallpaper bought for the hallway up in the dining room. *(Score fifteen points)*

The finer points

What I have talked about so far are the rudimentary stages of wallpapering, and I do hope I've given you a few tips on how to make life easier for yourself.

Now let's talk about those more difficult areas of wallpapering like trimming around a light switch, cutting round a ceiling rose or deftly dodging an ornate window frame, which one cannot always successfully ignore.

How does the bodger cope with these troublesome and demanding tasks?

Basically, he doesn't. With every generation of bodgers the simple rules still apply.

Figure 15

What repeat pattern?

Figure 16

Wallpapering round a light switch

Figure 17

Wallpapering round a ceiling rose

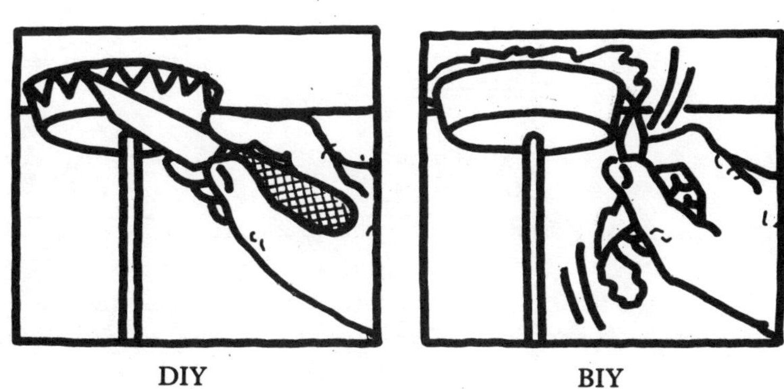

1. Don't worry about papering over, you can always cut your way out of the problem.
2. If you can't cut one piece of paper to go around the obstruction, use six.
3. Always blame it on the pattern.

Here to help you further are some hints on the type of problems you will find yourself with.

To save time and tempers when wallpapering, you should not only make no attempt to match patterns, etc., but should also ignore anything in your way. By papering over any object that doesn't move you will find that pipes, light switches, thermostats, ventilation ducts, grandfather clocks, pictures, etc., will all blend in smoothly with your overall scheme. One in the eye for Laura Ashley.

Once you've got into your stride, let nothing stand in your way. Carry out the act as quickly as possible until at least one of the three possibilities has been exhausted: the wall, the paper, the paste. Frequent stops during paperhanging are only allowed for liquid refreshment, ensuring that even if the paper doesn't get well and truly pasted, you do.

The following illustrations reveal a paperfolding technique perfected in the early fourteenth century by the brother of the famous Venetian explorer Marco Polo (the bodging traveller who never quite knew where he was going). Marco taught this specialised folding method to the Orientals he encountered on his journeys in return for the secret of sweet and sour pork. The Chinese promptly renamed the process Origami, which literally means 'game for a laugh'. Many rewarding hours of fun can be had prior to hanging the wallpaper by using the Origami method.

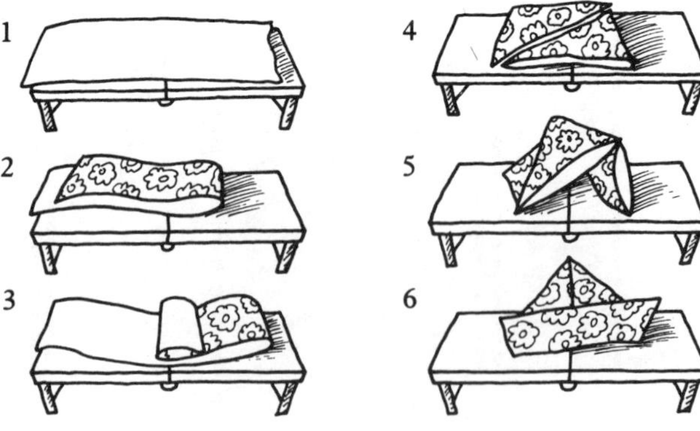

Figure 18

PLUMBING

There was a time when even normal folk wouldn't touch a simple plumbing job with a bargepole (theirs or anybody else's).

The old lead piping materials meant that a proficient DIYer, let alone a bodger, was quite capable of ensuring enough damp patches to grow a fine crop of mushrooms two floors up. All this is now changing, however, with the development of pipes and joints made in easier-to-bodge materials.

With the advent of plastic and copper tubing, the bodging plumber is in a position to take advantage of a full range of self-expression which would have previously been thought out of the question: the most legitimate reason for tearing the entire house apart and all with the jolly old Memsahib's blessing. Goodness gracious.

The British, if the truth be known, have always had a great affinity with water. Being surrounded by the stuff may have something to do with it. And no one enjoys water more than the bodger (except, of course, when he discovers unacceptable quantities of it in his beer).

In any event, an extensive study amongst bodgers the length and breadth of Britain's brewery chains has found that, unlike woodworking, plumbing is a science with its roots deep in the heart of the ballcock.

Perhaps one of the reasons why plumbing enjoys such great popularity, more so than other interesting forms of BIY, is that it totally mystifies the wife and even the precocious offspring. The extent of the poor woman's knowledge of the subject usually extends to being able to turn on the tap and nothing more – leaving her at your mercy.

Any bodger worth his weight in compression joints can gain many joyous hours away from the verbal slings and arrows of domestic life by playing the pipes. So, armed with a hammer, two spanners, snorkel, flippers, and his trusty six-pack, our happy bodger can retire to the attic confident that a quick 'I'm going to look at that ballcock on the cold water tank, dear . . . I think it's worked loose again' will gain him a couple of hours alone to ponder the wonders of the brewing industry or the intricacies of soccer.

Tapping a pipe every five minutes should banish any thoughts of slouching from the wife's mind. Should she wish to join your little expedition into the wet and slippery unknown, a mention of the likelihood of a dead bird in the tank will have her scurrying back to the kitchen before you can say Barry Bucknell.

Once you've learnt the basics of a simple plumbing wheeze you can develop your new-found talents on longer ones of say three or four days. One useful tip to remember is that when doing any form of plumbing, most Jim'll Fixits advise disconnecting the mains water supply from the existing system at the very last moment.

This is very sound advice, for example, if you are going to fit a new kitchen. Pick up any DIY manual and it will suggest you install your new sink completely, working backwards from there and connecting the mains at the very last minute. This will ensure that if any problems do crop up you can still use the old sink while the fault is being corrected.

However when has anyone with any imagination ever paid any attention to sound advice? The clever BIYer will sever the mains supply first, making sure he has some water in the kettle for a cuppa, naturally.

A couple of hours of looking as if you know what you're doing will call for some tremendous acting ability. (I suggest you read my *Is This a Hacksaw I See Before Me – A BIY Guide to Acting the Part.*)

Assuming that you have started your plumbing bodge on a Saturday afternoon your couple of hours' stalling will have seen you past the shop closing deadline. Now comes an Oscar-winning performance of a man sorely cheated by circumstance. Utter a few well-chosen expletives and announce to the cruel world that you have run out of olives (no, no you fool, not the ones you put in cocktails, compression joint olives). Having already cut off the water, the house will now remain waterless until the shops open again on Monday morning. This will mean making the supreme sacrifice of holding the fort while you pack the wife and little ones off to mother's for the duration.

Once the family is off down the road you can sit back and face your hideous ordeal with only the racing on the telly, a copious quantity of six-packs and a takeaway to comfort you. The wife will phone on Sunday to find out how you're getting on. Of course, you will be missing her terribly and praying for the day that water is restored to your little homestead.

Pigs could fly.

BASIC PLUMBING

Before we go any further with this section a strong word of warning is necessary to any bodger about to spread his water wings: consult your estate agent first.

It is one thing to bodge plumbing and quite another to have to live with it. Hope springs eternal in every bodger's life, and so does the leak from that little job he did a year ago. So do your worst, but leave it to some other soul to pick up the pieces and plug up the holes. The bodger's philosophy concerning plumbing is based on that old seafaring saying 'a rat never returns to a sinking ship' or, in this case, house. So, unless you've decided to slick back your hair, hold an orange peel in your teeth and take up synchronised swimming or fancy yourself as another Jacques Cousteau, start looking for another place to live.

Most plumbing manuals begin by boring the wetsuit off you with the life history of the entire English water system. All you really need to know, however, is that mains pressure and electric pumps take water up, and that gravity brings it down. After it has flowed around the system for a bit it comes out of a tap marked hot or cold.

It is extremely unlikely that a DIY man will ever come face to face with a house that needs replumbing from top to bottom. And any bodger who attempted such a task would be courting disaster such as the world and Acacia Avenue have never seen. So I've decided to address my grey matter to explaining the sorts of jobs that most bodgers would find well within their capabilities (or should I say just beyond them).

Changing a washer

You're probably thinking that there is no way anyone could bodge up such a simple task as this. Wrong.

Have you ever met the bodger who forgot to turn off the water supply before unscrewing the tap? Or what about a common bodging practice, that of using the wrong size spanner? It will remove the nut so that you can replace the washer and return the nut. Unfortunately it will also smooth down the gripping surface of the nut so badly that anyone attempting its removal again would be forced to question your parenthood.

But perhaps the most subtle bodge is achieved when the bodger, in a rush not to miss a second's drinking time at the Dog and Duck, puts the wrong tap handles on the wrong outlets. Thus hot comes out cold, and vice versa. This will also give the bodger hours of harmless fun observing unsuspecting guests trying to wash their hands. Naturally, the accomplished bodger will be able to explain this mishap by claiming that the taps are marked in accordance with their country of manufacture, Yugoslavia, and that they are, in fact, victims of the latest EEC regulations.

Washing machines, tumble-driers

While these white and chromium marvels of modern technology have relieved the housewife of washday drudgery, they have at the same time removed for many one of this country's greatest institutions: the launderette.

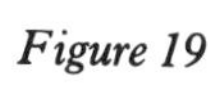
Figure 19

DIY BIY

Gone are the days when you would be despatched to the launderette with the washing only to stuff the same into the machine and pop across the road to the pub for a couple of hours' relaxation. At the local wash-'n'-rinse a chap could catch up on all the local gossip and discover whether that buxom brunette at the end of the street was getting more than just Gold Top from the milkman. And who could fail to get a lump in the throat at the thought of those young lovers in the Peckham Rye Washerama watching their smalls meet, touch, entangle and finally part all during a climactic forty-minute cycle. It used to beat the hell out of watching television.

But, unfortunately, washing machines and tumble-driers are here to stay and you will be required to give them your attention at some time.

It is extremely unlikely that the missus will insist on one of those machines that you just plug in and put the waste pipe into the sink. No, you'll be swiftly steered towards the white goods section of your local Currys and forced to purchase one with more moving parts than a Formula One racing car.

Once you've got the appliance in the house, use the illustrations above to give you a few ideas about the right way to plumb it in. It's worth mentioning here that no one of my acquaintance has ever successfully hooked up a washer-drier combination without causing at least one major flood and a minor fire.

It should make running down to the Ganges for a quick bit of stonewashing sound like bliss to even the most modern housewife.

Fitting a shower

Showers are part of modern life.

It used to be beer and skittles and tin baths, but today it's aerobics, jogging, young executives, biorhythms and showers.

DIY manuals give some excellent advice on the subject of fitting them, and one of their suggestions is to fit a shower outside the standard bathroom, in the corner of a bedroom – ensuite, as it were – or in a small downstairs room. A very practical idea, indeed. Saves all that queuing in the morning.

All you have to do to turn this practical suggestion into an impractical one is to ignore the section in all plumbing books that talks about something called *head of water*. With this one simple measure, you can have all the family and house guests limboing in the shower desperately trying to get the shower head in a position where it gives more than just a trickle of water. Needless to say, without observing the head of water rule, the pressure will never be quite enough to drown an ant (see Figure 20).

Of course, you can now acquire showers which are electrically heated. Thumb through the colour supplements on any Sunday and you'll see advertisements showing tastefully naked ladies enjoying the benefits of these handy little gadgets. A word of warning. Because the water supply has to be connected to the unit, which is then coupled up to the mains supply, I suggest that this is one occasion when you should join the shy and nervous and let an expert fit the unit. However, once that is done, there is no reason why the playful bodger shouldn't complicate things in the new shower room by fitting pullcord light switches next to the new pullcord shower switch. Then add a pullcord for the window blinds. With more cords hanging down than vines in a Tarzan movie, anyone stepping into the new shower for the first time is bound to wildly pull a cord, and unexpectedly find themselves in the dark, running hot and cold, or exposed to the neighbours.

Perhaps you already know somebody who is into this form of campanology? Does it ring any bells?

Figure 20

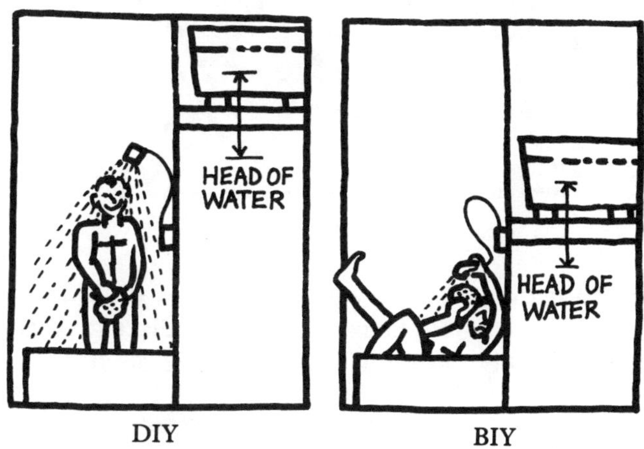

Downstairs cloakroom, fitting a sink

The great status symbol used to be having two cars, but these days two loos (no, not the shorthand French painter) are the order of the day.

The downstairs cloakroom has developed into a second home for the smallest room in the house. You too can join the élite by adding washing facilities to your downstairs loo, thus creating a feature guaranteed to bring a smile to any estate agent's lips.

While it is easy to install such fittings there are a few essential points to remember. As my illustration shows, you must first find a sink that is far too large for the cloakroom and position it so that the door can't be opened more than eleven inches. This will ensure that no single-jointed, non-yoga practising, two-legged mammal can possibly sit on the toilet for more than a few moments without getting an excruciating attack of cramp.

A relatively easy form of cloakroom bodging, perfect for pompous dinner guests, is the 'Oh God, I forgot to put the u-bend back on the cloakroom sink' routine. Picture the scene as your guest returns red-faced to the table with dulled patent shoes and soapy water in his turn-ups. Imagine the effect on a pair of hush puppies.

Figure 21

Try the old u-bend trick next time you have people around. You won't have to ask them again. Instead you'll be invited to their place to empty their drinks cabinet for a change. But be careful if they too have a downstairs washroom.

Figure 22 The old u-bend trick

Bodgers come from a broken home

Hunt the Stopcock

It's an odd DIY fact that few people know where to turn when an emergency hits their homes, especially when they've just moved in.

When the power fails, for instance, the first hour is spent in the dark recesses looking for anything that may resemble a fuse box, or a box of candles.

When the water starts coming through the roof it's all hands to the pumps and pass the bucket. (However, in a bodger's home most of the buckets have more holes in them than the roof.)

And of course, when there's a leak in the water system, the household goes mad looking for any tap that might stop the deluge.

Hunt the Stopcock is a game designed to let the bodger enjoy getting his feet wet – in a manner of speaking. The game is based on the premise that as a bodger you will have no idea where the stopcock is in your house. Even if you did have this priceless piece of information, it would do you little good. Stopcocks are hard to find at the best of times. But a true bodger can make them as difficult to track down as the Abominable Snowman.

Essential pipework is invariably hidden behind secret wall panels or rather rashly concreted over. Boilers are placed in such awkward places that even the Gas Board won't touch them. All things are done so as to induce a state of panic as you watch your furniture running downstream and out of the house.

With Hunt the Stopcock the only headless chickens are the ones you play with. So try your hand at the game that's full of thrills and spills. For once you've got nothing to lose.

Hunt the stopcock

The game that puts you in the swim of things without getting your feet wet.

How to play

This is a game for up to 4 players.

Each player places his headless chicken on the START square and throws the two dice.

The player who throws the highest score goes first, the second highest next, and so on.

You must throw the exact number required to land on the final square.

If there is an overthrow (not an overflow) you must go back as many spaces.

The first player to finish the course and find the stopcock loses.

It is the player who by sheer bodger's cunning completes the course last who wins.

A player who after five hours still hasn't ended up on square 36 shall be crowned Grandmaster.

Cock up

To make this game as lifelike as possible we have included a few 'dirty curve' squares called COCK UPs. Land on one and you have a choice. . . .

1. Be chicken and move back two squares, or . . .

2. Throw six or less with your two dice. If you succeed you may go back six squares. If you fail you must go forward six squares. Cock up!

Cut out and colour your 4 headless chickens.

36 THE STOPCOCK YOU LOSE!!

35

25 CEILING COLLAPSES UNDER WEIGHT OF WATER. GO DOWN TO 13

26

24

23 YOU FIND ADJUSTAB SPANNER.PROC TO NO 28

13

14

12 COCK UP

11

1 THE LEAK STARTS HERE

2

34
33
COCK UP
32 ANOTHER LEAK. TERRIFIC PLAY. RETURN TO SQUARE 1.
31
27
YOU FIND THE PLUMBING PLANS FOR THE HOUSE! GO TO NO 34
28
29
30 YOU FIND A STOPCOCK BUT IT'S THE WRONG ONE........ PHEW! BACK TO 18
OCK UP
21
20
19
MOUSE HOLE FOR SALE
A DUTCHMAN
CALLS AND PUTS
INGER ON THE
BLEM. BAD
.. HAVE
THER
16
YOU FIND A STOPCOCK. UNFORTUNATELY IT FALLS OFF IN YOUR HANDS. BACK TO 9
17
18
COCK UP
STOPCOCK IS FOUND, BUT IT'S THE WRONG ONE. GO TO NO 7
10
9
8
IRATE NEIGHBOUR TELLS YOU WATER IS POURING INTO HIS LIVING ROOM. WELL DONE. MISS A GO.
7
THE WIFE
TTEMPTS TO
ALL IN A
LUMBER. GO
TO 31.
3
4
5
6

Spaghetti Junction

Once again we are indebted to Richard Rogers, the British architect who masterminded the Paris Arts Centre, for bringing plumbing out into the open in a big way.

Of course, it makes perfect sense to put pipes where you can see them. This saves you from making the mistake of putting a nail through them next time you want to rehang your Boots copy of the Mona Lisa in green.

And just imagine the thrill and satisfaction of seeing your handiwork in all its glory, with pipes running down, along and across the wall, each painted in a different exciting colour. Picture the beauty of a room where a 22mm diameter domestic copper pipe meanders from skirting board to cornice without the slightest hint of an apology. Consider the appeal of a diagonal pipe with stopcock dominating your living room. Or the elegance of a fine 15mm branch line snaking around your mantelpiece.

Here are a few of the better-known variations to give you the idea.

Figure 23a *Stop tap with 22mm in horizontal hold . . . stunning*

Figure 23b *Double 90° capillary with 15mm . . . nice*

Figure 23c A three-piece in the living room . . . sweet

Joints

When displaying your worst, it's best to have a few tricks up your copper sleeve.

The joining of two pipes can be very easily accomplished with compression joints. However, bodgers are awarded no marks for artistic compression or technical merit. So avoid their use.

Figure 24

Capillary joints are much more difficult to master, but a lot of fun when you have. And, armed with a blowtorch and liberal amounts of solder a boring joint can be turned into a piece of art. Whether you favour Epstein, Frink, Rodin or Moore, sculpt a masterpiece soon.

However, if you feel that your pipework doesn't really merit a showing at the Tate just yet you can have nearly as much fun hiding it under the floorboards. Here are a few tips that are sure to make your successor's life a little soggier.

Cut into the joists as deeply as possible (see Figure 25). This will, firstly, allay any fears the wife might have about you putting a nail through the pipe again. Secondly, weaken the floor so much that the wife will no longer be able to hold her Tuesday Weight Watchers meeting in your house.

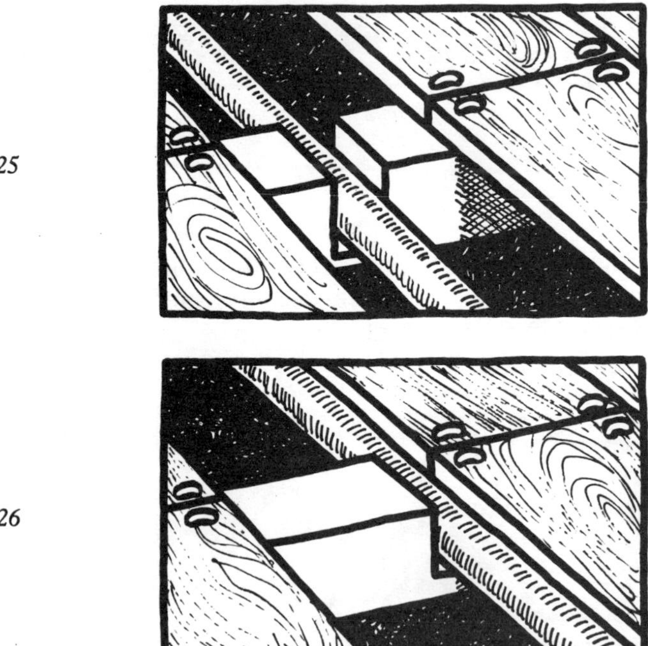

Figure 25

Figure 26

When running pipes under the flooring, avoid putting them through the middle of the joist. Instead, position them to the left or right (see Figure 26). Make sure when you've placed the floorboards back that you don't put a nail through a pipe yourself. Leave that particular trick to the next unfortunate occupant who attempts to mend a loose floorboard with a six-inch nail.

BIY

WOODWORK

Wood. Just keep repeating the word for a minute or two and you'll almost be able to taste it. Wood is God's material.

And yet, it takes Mother Nature fifty years' hard work to get a mighty oak from a little acorn and just five minutes for some chap from Texas with a chain saw to bring it down again.

Wood saved Noah from getting a soaking. And it provided just the dark horse the Greeks needed to win at Troy.

Such wonderful things are made from wood (cricket bats, snooker cues, golf clubs, beer barrels). And now it's our material, the stuff bodges are made of. Generation after generation has produced great things out of wood and now it's your turn to let future generations look at your efforts and say with pride, 'That was a right bodge-up.'

Old chums will be able to look back over the years while supping their pints in the Carpenter's Arms, regaling each other with stories of bodging prowess . . . 'Do you remember '85, the bedroom cabinets . . . and what about '81 and the sash windows . . . ar, those were the days all right . . . they don't make bodges like that any more.'

Wood has always had a special place in the heart of the bodger. Ever since the invention of the square wheel, wood has played an important part in the success of bodging enterprises.

The first step on the road to ruin with wood for you begins with a trip to your local timber yard. Just follow your nose in and out of the stacks of two-by-ones and four-by-twos until you feel comfortable with this wonderful grainy stuff. Run your fingers through the barrels of nails. Check out the cornices and mouldings, and watch how your fellow browsers behave in this sacred place. Soon you'll be able to tell a BIYer from a DIYer with only a glance.

The easiest place to spot the difference is in the car park. Here the DIY people will be zipping about in their Volvo estates, the backs of their cars groaning with everything required for a weekend's work. What they can't get in the back goes neatly on the roof rack.

The bodger, of course, sticks out a mile (quite literally). He's the one who's bought fourteen nine-feet lengths of two-by-one, six four feet by four feet sheets of three-quarter-inch chipboard, four pounds of wire nails and eighteen packs of wood filler, all of which he is now trying to stuff into the back of his ancient Morris 1100.

There'll be lengths of wood coming out of every window of his car and his front passenger seat is so laden with wood filler that there's no way he's going to be able to get the gear lever into second.

Back in the timber yard, you should by now be feeling relaxed about your new environment and ready to get to grips with some of the varieties of wood you see before you.

Warped. Scuffed. Twisted. Knotted.

No, this isn't a casual reference to the mother-in-law. I am talking wood. You will find that the worse condition a piece of wood is in, the cheaper it will be. As most wood you use for home projects will wind up covered in one way or another (with paint, or rugs, or the complete Charles Dickens), there is no point in paying for perfection.

Hardwoods, softwoods, blockwoods, plywoods, chipboards, oak, ash or pine – which one to choose? This is the question that faces the DIYer and one that will worry him for days. The bodger, on the other hand, will simply pick up the nearest piece of wood and not concern himself whether or not he's got the right wood for the job. Suitability, schmootability. The bodger skates majestically through all the rules like Torvill and Dean. Often knocking up the quick garden shed in chipboard or using the finest cabinetmaker's English oak to produce a rather stylish, if somewhat wonky, workbench for the garage. Eat your heart out, Chippendale.

The ingenuity and skill of the bodger lies in the fact that he'll take anything that is quick and cheap to use. He will then apply his creative brain to ways of making up for the shortfall in materials and manpower. A DIYer, however, will hide behind quality tools and materials.

While you're in the yard you may as well get acquainted with your future adversary – the sales assistant. It is essential that you stamp your authority on the counter from the outset. That you do not let him intimidate you.

For, after all, it is a contest of wills which you are fighting. A matter of principles. Will you submit to his attitude that the customer is always wrong? Will you stand meekly in line with DIYers waiting to be embarrassed about your lack of knowledge concerning the life and times of the countersink drill, 1583 to 1985? Will you mumble indecisively when questioned on the slightest technical term by our now mocking assistant?

A good bodger won't, by George.

With the right mental attitude a bodger can have hours of fun in the company of unwary sales assistants, who, perhaps unkindly, have been credited as the source of the expression 'as thick as two short planks'.

First of all, refuse to communicate with them in their own language, preferring your own description of a skirting board as 'one of those long bits that goes at the bottom of the wall', or your summing up of a few lengths of tongue and groove as 'Lego for grown-ups'.

Once you've got the poor chap well and truly baffled, ask him to cut your selected pieces of wood into lots of different lengths. Like the wood, this should cut him down to size. And just before the distraught sales assistant makes his first pencil mark on the virgin wood for cutting, become vague and inject the phrase 'no . . . just add a couple of inches, but perhaps there again . . .'

Indecisions, indecisions.

THE GOLDEN RULES

Wood, being one of the finer substances of life, requires careful and precise handling, which in turn demands careful and precise measuring.

Poppycock.

Before a hammer is raised, a saw drawn, a plank planed or a thumb hit, a bodger can stamp his authority and his name on a piece of woodwork. Throw away your Black & Decker retractable rule, eject your plumb line, jettison your spirit level and discard your mitre block.

Wood requires much more natural means of measurement and shaping. Here is where the 'rule of thumb' and 'true eye' rule OK.

Follow your eye and your thumb to the ends of the living room. Boldly bodge where no man has bodged before. Delve into the outer limits.

My guide to measurements in the home opens up a whole new world to the

Figure 27

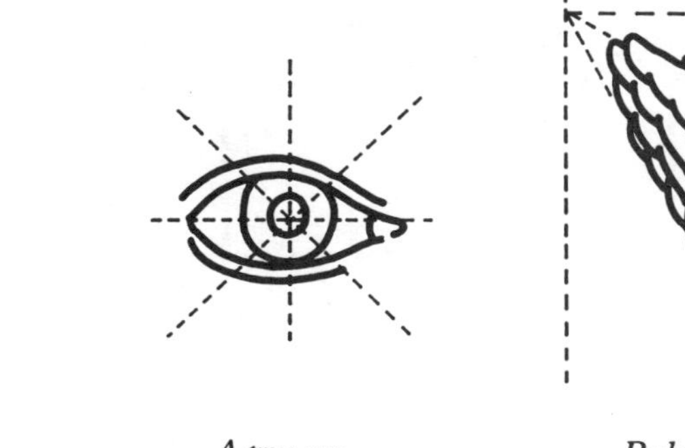

A true eye

Rule of thumb

devil-may-care, confident, 'no contraptions' bodger.

May the force (and the Building Society) be with you.

Physical measurements can be useful in certain circumstances, but being too accurate puts too much constraint on both your material and your design. Measure for flexibility. My system also avoids encumbering yourself with the plethora of pencils, rulers, pens and paper (that the DIYers seem so fond of) which always seem to go missing just when you need them most. In fact, for those days when your eyes are difficult enough to open let alone register any form of distance, I've devised an easy-to-use system of measurement that requires no tools.

Figure 28

The Pincer Movement (for measurements of between 4 and 6 inches at a pinch)

The Sleepwalker (a dream of a technique that gives you 36 inches at a stretch)

The Big 'E' (from elbow to fingertip, a leisurely 18 inches)

The Albatross (spread your wings for a full measure of approx. 5 feet – if you're 6 feet tall – and pray for a happy landing)

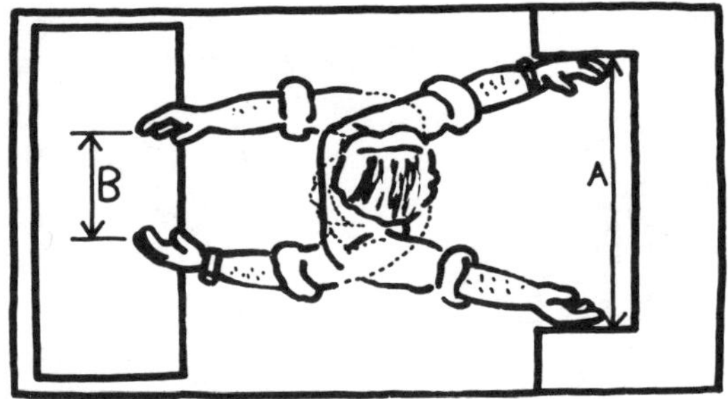

Figure 29 How to measure an alcove

The 'What the eye can't see' method

It is often said that beauty is in the eye of the beholder. This phrase has often been used to great effect by bodging woodworkers in defence of their results.

Non-bodgers have a way of not understanding this and immediately launching into monologues on finishing techniques and the value of a cabinet being no greater than the legs it stands on or the ability of its drawers to open.

Every practised bodger knows, however, that a couple of well-placed louvred doors can cover a multitude of sins – not to mention hundreds of cracked batons, wayward nails, bruised walls and pounds of wood filler oozing from crevices. Any finished project is no worse than its surface appearance. And that's a fact.

Figure 30

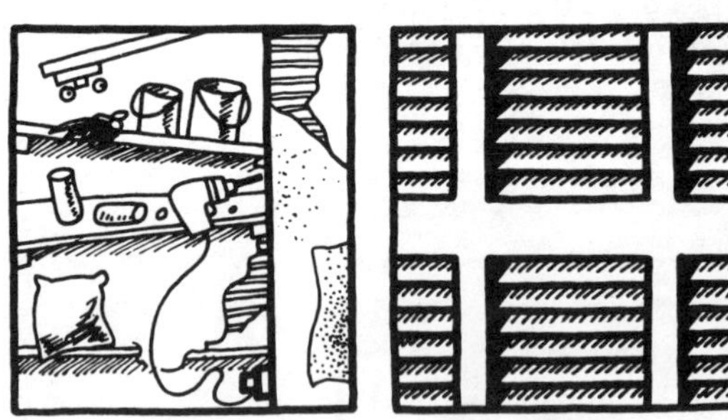

Now you see it *Now you don't*

This simple 'what the eye can't see' method can be extended through the whole house. Rooms where the walls are damp and cracked (the result of BIY plumbing?), the ceilings cracked and damp, can be miraculously transformed by a few lengths of tongue and groove, leaving only your successor with a hatful of problems.

A little cork board in the right place can hide the crumbling plaster or cover the spot where you used to hang the dartboard. Entire floors that are infested with woodworm and dry rot can be turned into a surface to shame the local bowling alley with a few sheets of trusty blockboard.

– THE GOLDEN RULES APPLIED –

We are now approaching that part of this section that concerns itself with the nitty gritty of bodge carpentry. To start the proceedings off on the right foot, an introduction to the bodger's two principal weapons is now required.

Figure 31 The Holy Nail

Here before you lies the patron saint of Bodging. Our hero's St Christopher. His lucky rabbit's foot. His mystical amulet. His saviour from a catastrophe of his own making.

The well-known and respected six-incher is capable of being used on any job large or small, from tacking a carpet to building a bookcase, making the screw completely obsolete.

In fact, there is virtually no problem – inside or outside the home – which the six-inch nail cannot solve. It's always worth having at least three or four dozen of these beauties spread around the house at all times. You never know when you might need them.

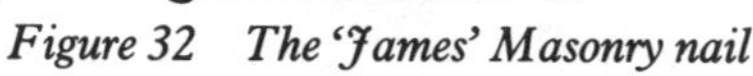

Figure 32 The 'James' Masonry nail

Quite frankly, any use of screws or rawlplugs is completely frowned upon and would cast grave doubts about your desire to 'come out of the closet' and join the cause. However, help is at hand.

The masonry nail is designed as a multi-purpose tool, able to go through wood, bricks, cement, copper piping and electric cables faster than a bodger through a pack of elastoplast.

With a varied selection of masonry nails at your disposal, a whole range of jobs requiring firm and permanent fixing to the wall, internal and external, can be done, with none of the fuss and complications and frustrated hours normally spent in trying to cut those little plastic cylinders into the right size.

Joints

To get anywhere in woodwork it is important to master the art of joining two pieces of wood together. This is called a joint. There are many types of joint achievable by the bodger, depending on his ability and their suitability to the job at hand.

As this is a beginner's book, however, I strongly advise sticking to the more elementary halving joint to start with. Once you've learnt how to cope with this tricky little customer you can go on to more adventurous types of joint.

In Figure 33 I show in simple detail the right way and the wrong way to tackle the halving joint.

Armed with your trusty tenon saw, wood glue, a few six-inchers and plenty of wood filler, see how close you can get to the finish shown in the illustration.

When sawing wood it is important to follow the 'Rule of Thumb' technique. This means that the use of the instruments I described earlier in this section is definitely out.

Following are a number of the methods commonly used among the knowledgeable which not only hold two pieces of wood together but give a clue to the imagination, creativity and personality of their inventor. Try a few out and see which joint you feel most at home with. Or devise a fool-proof system of your own.

Figure 33

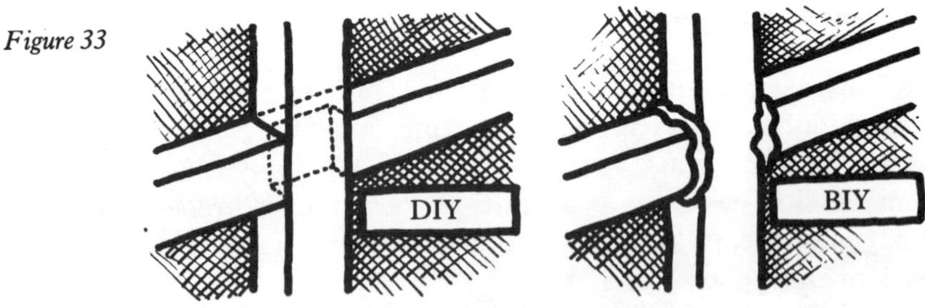

A simple halving joint

Figure 34

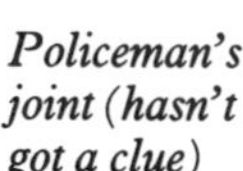

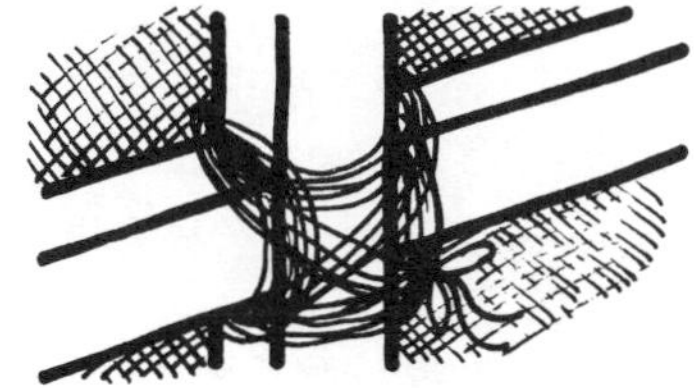

Policeman's joint (hasn't got a clue)

Traveller's joint (always needs a lot of packing)

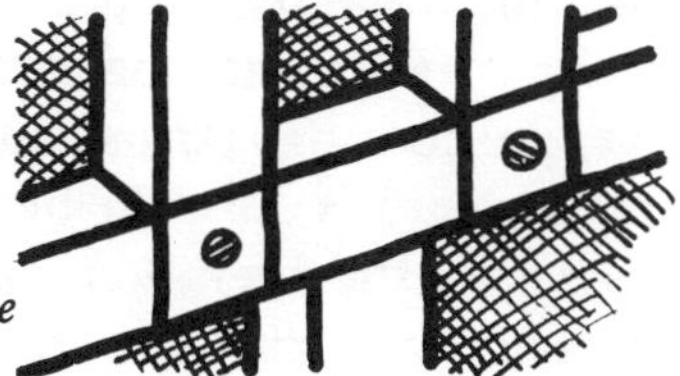

Bigamist's joint (twice the trouble and strife)

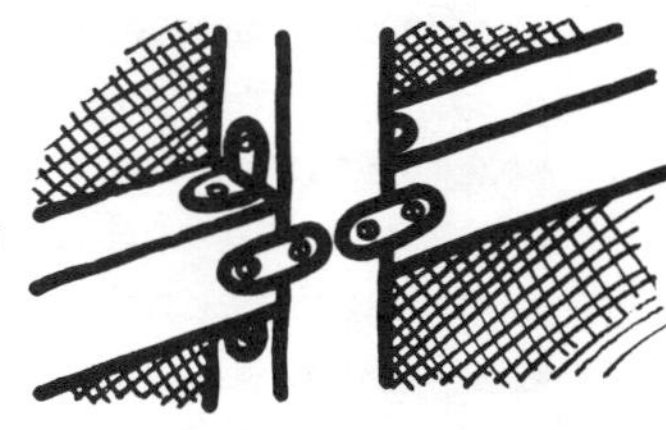

Insurance man's joint (every angle covered)

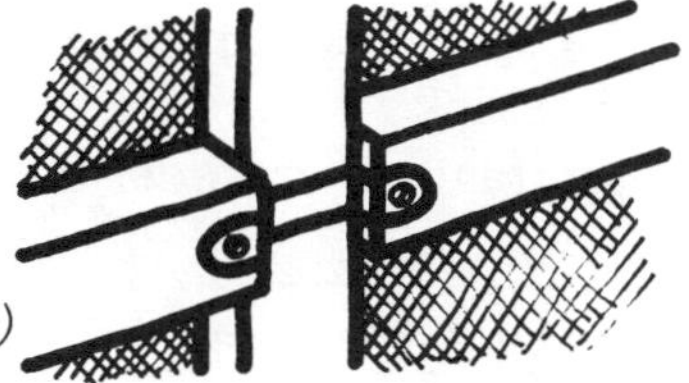

MP's joint (it's always in recess)

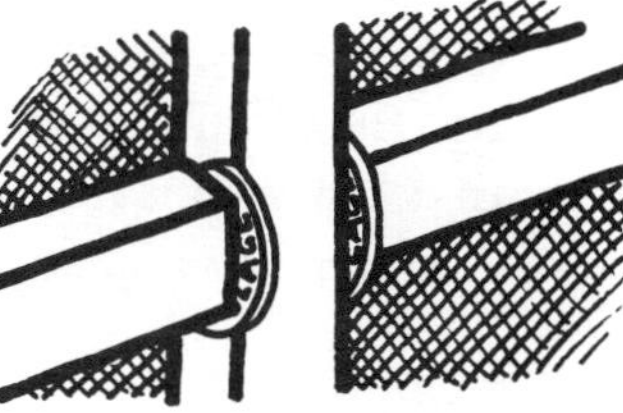

Publican's joint (he always likes to see his joint well packed)

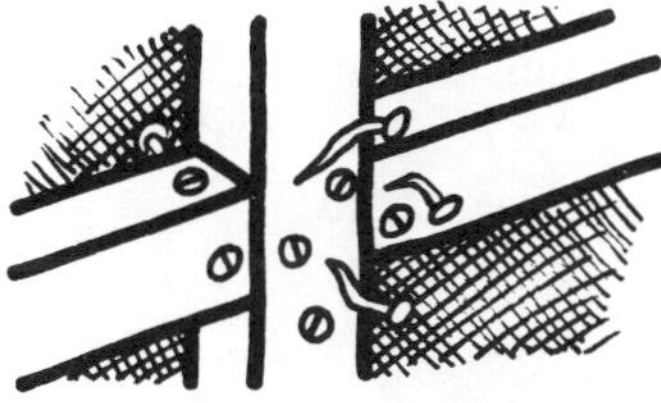

Gambler's joint (never knows when to stop)

Pilot's joint (only held up on a wing and a prayer)

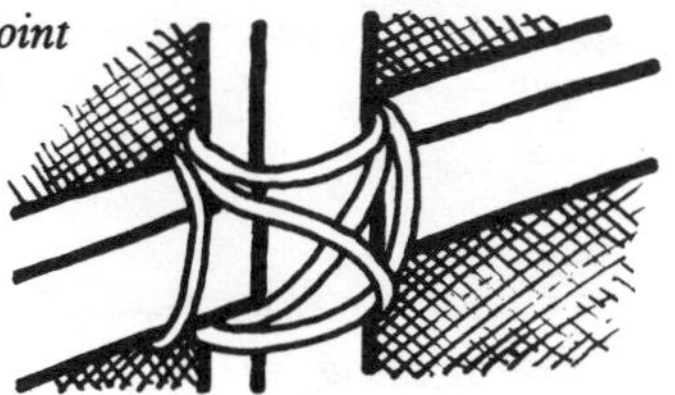

Civil servant's joint (all wrapped up in red tape)

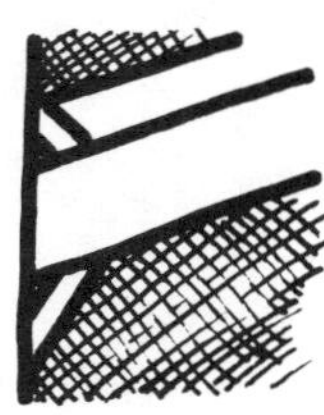

Dolly Parton joint (always in need of some extra support)

Sawing

Sawing is one woodworking activity that can be carried out in any part of the house. Even if the shavings and dust are trodden into the wife's favourite carpet they're easy enough to hoover up at the end of the week.

You need only four things to start sawing: a piece of wood, a chair or flat surface (the new kitchen work surface would be an ideal spot) on which to rest the former, a saw, and a spare hand to hold the wood securely.

Having first marked your wood on one side, saw in a fast and furious manner, stopping frequently for refreshment. There is nothing intrinsically interesting or character-building about sawing, so the sooner it's done the better.

If you get either carried away with this part of the operation, or so plastered that you inadvertently saw through the chair or work surface as well, don't worry. It's what's known as an occupational hazard.

Once the wood has been cut, the rough edges (and there will be plenty of them) will need smoothing down with sandpaper. If sandpaper is not available, rub the offending edges against a convenient brick wall (making sure, of course, that this wall is not of your own making lest it fall down under the pressure).

Rome could have been built in a day

Simple jobs

Armed with a saw and some wood, the bodger can create all kinds of useful and exotic items for the home. Here are just some of them.

The three-legged coffee table

Not only does this design reduce the amount of marking that coffee tables do to the carpet, but it also provides a fascinating topic of after-dinner conversation.

The detachable shelf

So designed for easy removal (either by you as a consequence of too much weight or by vibrations caused by a passing hedgehog).

The continental shelf

This neat row of shelves is designed not to be able to take those nasty little gifts people bring you back from holidays. You know, things like models of the Eiffel Tower in the snow and lighters in miniature ski boots.

Instead, our heroic row of shelves will only take a certain size and thickness of book. Your twenty-five editions of Wisden's cricket almanack, for instance, will fit more snugly than a cricket box.

Howzat!

The kitchen table

The standard four-legged kitchen table made in pine is not beyond the capabilities of the average bodger. Some people say they have trouble getting the leg lengths even, but there isn't really any need to be too finicky. The very worst that can happen is that you are left with a table at the perfect height for a Japanese dinner party. Immediately clinching your reputation as a neighbourhood trend-setter.

The coat rack

Another simple gem. Just a piece of wood, some ready made aluminium coat hooks from Woolies (the ones that snap off after a little use will do) and a supply of the famous six-inch nail.

The wine rack

A wine rack is one of the few home projects that deserves to be treated seriously. After all, it does touch on a subject close to everyone's heart.

When it comes to making your wine rack, size is all important. None of this namby-pamby couple of bottles of Muscatel, some nondescript supermarket plonk, a bottle of Nuit St Georges and the rest of the spaces reserved for the next delivery of undrinkable Beaujolais Nouveau. I am talking bulk; I am talking wine lake.

Take the basic construction based on those models you'll find in all good 'all pine' shops and enlarge on it.

If you have a spare room, enlarge it to fit the spare room. If you have a basement, enlarge it to fit the basement.

When the wife complains, point out the obvious advantages: less area to dust, a smaller area of wall to decorate and the increasing investment value of your 144 bottles of Chateau Cape Canaveral.

Votre santé, Houston.

PABLO PICASSO

It would be a great injustice if I were to finish this chapter on woodworking without a mention of one of the most famous bodging carpenters of all time.

I refer, of course, to Pablo Picasso (1892–1980), the creator of Cubism.

When this acknowledged genius wasn't slapping another masterpiece on to canvas he liked nothing more than a gentle spot of carpentry. So proud of his woodwork was he, in fact, that much of it crept into his paintings. In fact it was BIY that first gave the young Pablo the idea for Cubism.

Despite what the experts may have read into Picasso's distorted, twisted, ill-balanced furniture in his paintings, they were not a result of the artist's search for truth and the meaning of life. Pablo was painting exactly what he saw, and probably whistled cheerfully as he did so.

But artists of the day began copying his style of painting and Cubism gained international recognition. However, if the art world had only taken the time to pay a visit to Pablo's home they would have seen the error of their ways (not to mention some of Pablo's errors on the old carpentry front).

Nobody's perfect

GENERAL JOBS AROUND THE HOME

Thus far, I have tried to give you some sound advice on specific tasks that you will be confronted with from time to time. Now I'd like to concentrate on the myriad little jobs you can expect to be thrown your way. Each of these jobs, tasks, projects, ordeals (call them what you will) requires different talents.

So, rather than swamp you with a plethora of information about each, I've split this section into two parts. The first deals with what is commonly known as the famous five-minute job; and the second section concentrates on the more complicated.

A good bodger always blames his tools

THE FAMOUS FIVE-MINUTE JOB

Every Saturday morning, thousands of men happily come down to breakfast and the prospect of three Shredded Wheat, only to be confronted with the dreaded five-minute job. You know the sort of thing I mean: the loose lock, the promised spice shelf, the renegade bathroom tiles, the light fixture that's been sitting in its box for three months. The trick with the five-minute job, of course, is that it rarely takes less than an entire weekend to complete.

Remember the time the wife asked you to fit a new ornate brass letterbox on the front door, and you wound up with a twelve-inch cat flap, three feet off the ground? Or the problem with the sticking door which you solved so efficiently that it now only closes when locked? Or the Saturday you decided to put a quick coat of emulsion on the bathroom wall and two weeks later you were still putting in the new sink?

These are the sort of jobs which, if you're not careful, can take over your life entirely. To avoid this, it is necessary to get them into some kind of perspective. Are you going to be controlled by a bunch of Boy Scout projects? Or are you going to control them?

Imaginationless soft-touch that he is, the DIYer will of course choose the former, belting through his chores for the day at a speed that would make the proverbial rat up a drainpipe look positively sluggish. Putting an undercoat on a skirting board at first light, he will bleed all the radiators in the central heating system, put another coat of paint on the skirting board, mow the lawn, clean the car, repair the wobbly banister rail and put another coat of paint on the blessed skirting board and all before he cooks lunch in the microwave he built himself from scratch.

The BIYer, on the other hand, has realised the hidden catch of that particular situation. It can be likened to one of those computer games where the more of those little spaceships you blow up, the more of the little beggars arrive on the horizon.

The bodger selects the *one* five-minute job that appeals to him most (which is to say, the one that is least horrifying) and sets about it in a leisurely fashion, determined to make the job last as long as possible so that no other five-minute job can be squeezed in before the sun sets. Easy, isn't it? Not completely. It does require a bit of effort to concoct enough excuses to keep the wife off the scent and blissfully ignorant of the ploy.

For example, the tap has been dripping in the bathroom for two months now and today is the day you've elected to rectify the fault. After whipping the top off the tap you discover (oh horrors!) that you need a rare type of washer, and you'll have to travel all the way to the plumber's merchant to find one. Five hours later . . . Getting the idea?

I've completed a little chart of just some of the most common five-minute jobs you are likely to come up against, and have also included some excuses to go with them. Of course, it's always best if you can think up one of your own, but you can use the chart to help you time your own performance and compare it to the bodging standards you must strive for in the future.

'5-minute job'	**DIY time**	**Pre-BIY time**	**Post-BIY time**	**Failsafe**
Changing a washer on the bathroom tap	20 mins	½ day	1 day	'Common Market washer sizes'
Repair of squeaky floorboard	1 hour	5 hours	12 hours	'Looking for a mouse'
Clothes rail in the wardrobe	20 mins	3 hours	5 hours	'Modern clothes too heavy'
Coat hook on the bathroom door	10 mins	3 hours	4 hours	'Still looking for bathroom door'
Curtain rail	1 hour	5 hours	1 day	'What's wrong with Venetian blinds?'
Putting new plug on iron	5 mins	1hour	2 hours	'New colour code very confusing'
A minor repair in the garden	1 hour	3 hours	1 day	'Been admiring the dahlias'
Unblocking the kitchen sink	2 hours	1 day	4 days	'Waste disposal disposed of tools'
Putting a new bolt on the front door	½ hour	½ day	1 day	'Too much traffic'
Replacing a tile in the bathroom	½ hour	1 hour	3 hours	'The missing tile reduces condensation'
Fixing the wobbly leg on a table	20 mins	1 hour	5 hours	'We'll only have to buy something to put on it'
Putting up a new clothesline	40 mins	50 mins	2 hours	'The weatherman has forecast a high wind'
Bleeding a central heating radiator	5 mins	½ hour	2 hours	'The wife will miss the gurgling sound'

Replacing the stair rod	1 hour	1½ hours	5 hours	'I've run out of 6-inch nails'
Hanging a new picture	30 mins	1 hour	4 hours	'I'm still out of 6-inch nails'
Putting a new castor on a chair	30 mins	50 mins	3½ hours	'Got an anti-clockwise castor when I need a clockwise one'
Lagging the bathroom pipes	30 mins	1 hour	8 hours	'They're too hot to handle, wait till they cool down'
Fixing the sticky bedroom window of No. 1 son	1 hour	2 hours	4 hours	'The little darling might fall out'
Putting up a spice rack	1 hour	2½ hours	8 hours	'The marjoram makes you sneeze'
Putting hanging baskets in the conservatory	1 hour	4 hours	8 hours	'I've run out of 6-inch nails again'

MORE ADVANCED JOBS

Floors

Floors are hard to avoid. It is difficult to ignore them by simply closing your eyes every time you pass one; and impossible to put them out of your mind by sticking a large plant in front of them. It is, however, possible to put them out of your sight by covering them up.

Carpet laying

The simplest way of hiding a floor is by carpeting it. Many strong men panic at the thought of fitting their own carpets, and many others hold entire dinner parties in a trance-like state for hours while they explain in detail the complexities of carpeting a medium-sized room with fireplace and wall recesses. Both responses are exaggerated. There is nothing difficult about this job, it's merely a question of mind over matter.

The first thing to ask yourself when setting about a spot of creative carpet laying is: Who needs underlay? If you are replacing a carpet, your underlay is already in position. If you are carpeting a bare room, though, don't worry about underlay this time and it'll be there the next. Sceptics might assume that a refusal to use underlay shows a lack of initiative when in fact it is simply practical. Underlay not only muffles the creaks that might catch a burglar unawares, but also makes it impossible to detect the pitter patter of tiny feet heading your way on a Sunday morning.

When you select your carpet (or when your wife selects your carpet) ensure that it is large enough to easily fill the room. DIYers seem to enjoy nothing more than the challenge of stretching a carpet into every corner of the room, but we know better.

The first step is to empty the room of furniture (which, unfortunately, cannot be helped). Next, throw the carpet into the centre of the room, and then move your heaviest bits of furniture into the centre of the carpet. (You may need a fellow bodger to help you with this.) Then, slowly and evenly, slide the furniture from the centre of the carpet to its edges. A six-inch nail or two judiciously placed will hold it down for ever. Be careful when laying, however, that nothing comes between the deep pile and the floor. Otherwise, when the job is well and truly done and you are just on your way to the local to relax you may instead find yourself reflecting on the nature of the lump in the middle of the carpet as the wife asks, 'Where's Tiddles?'

Figure 35 Carpeting: the finishing touch

Nowadays, however, there are some interesting alternatives to carpeting which you might want to try:

Floor tiles

Laying floor tiles, be they plastic or carpet, is a snap. If you play your cards right, you don't even have to empty the room that you're tiling, but can cover it section by section, moving the furniture on to the newly placed tiles as you finish each section to ensure that they stay down. It is a waste of time bothering to prepare the floor with sanding and filler (it is going to be covered, after all); a little extra adhesive will take care of any holes or dents. You can also shave hours off your time by ignoring anything you've ever heard about marking out or dry tiling. One way or another, they'll fit in the end, and once you've got all the furniture back in place no one's going to notice what size the tiles along the wall are anyway. It should be remembered, though, that a gap between tiles aids in drainage, cleaning and general accessibility.

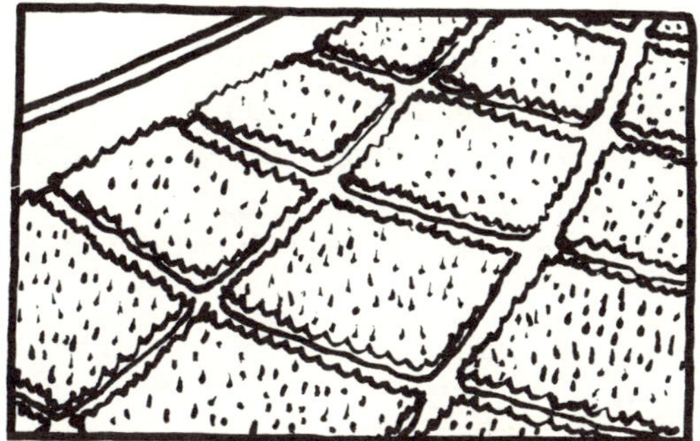

Figure 36 Carpet tiles: good game, good game

Rush matting

Just the name will appeal to the ardent bodger. Throw the matting on the floor and rush to the nearest pub.

Cushionfloor linoleum

More often than not you will cut this too short. Fear not, this particular product can be stretched to cover your shortcomings in the measurement department. As a bonus, you will have a floor with all the properties of an Olympic-standard trampoline.

General note

No matter what covering you choose, it will sooner or later come to your attention that there is no such thing as a perfectly square or perfectly rectangular room. Lurking around every corner you will find nooks and crannies, jutting fireplaces and radiators, etc. – each designed to complicate your life. Your only course of action is to ignore them completely. With carpet or tiles, you will have strips of excess material left over and can use that to fill in any unsightly gaps. This method will remain totally undetected until the wife and her hoover get wind of your little deception (see Figure 35).

Roofing

If your roof tiles start showering down like the proverbial cats and dogs, you may find that a few strips of unibond will come in very handy to plug the gaps between the remaining tiles. Especially if you just happen to buy unibond of a different colour to that of your roof. Over a period of winters, this will result in the effect of a giant unstarted crossword puzzle or a rather drab patchwork quilt. Either look is bound to send the wife through the roof you've just repaired.

As autumn leaves start to fall, you can be sure that she will not tolerate another winter bailing out the bedroom. You will be sent up on the roof to sort out the guttering.

Replacing the offending gutter sections with sections of that nice shiny plastic variety is a good idea but make sure that none of it is angled towards the drainage pipe. That way the day that the rains come down you'll be able to put on a display more impressive than the water gardens of Geneva or the Fountain di Trevi in Rome.

Bricklaying

Any experts (so I am told) can lay bricks quickly and well. The rest of us can generally do one or the other, but rarely both. Considering the general instability of the world today and the high number of automobiles that daily go through brick walls, I'd settle for quick.

Any type of bricklaying – whether a two-storey extension (heaven forbid) or a simple (there's that word again) low garden wall – starts with preparation. (On the question of foundations, refer to the Italian architect in the History section.)

The mixing of cement, however, is a different kettle of poussin entirely. This is the part of bricklaying that can take a chap back to his childhood and the many happy hours he spent on the beach at Frinton mixing buckets of sand with seawater until a beautiful and aesthetic texture was obtained. Apply the same principles to mixing cement, but first choose your spot. Always try and mix your cement where it will cause the most inconvenience (why should you be the only one to suffer?). On the patio where the wife holds her bridge club would be ideal.

Once your cement is mixed, your most important decision is what bond (this is a technical term for the pattern of laying the bricks) to use. Most of the bonds recommended in DIY manuals require a certain amount of planning and brick breaking. Brick breaking is time-consuming and tricky, and unless you were thinking of paving over the garden in brick fragments anyway I would avoid it. If you use plenty of mortar, the BIY bond in Figure 37 is more than adequate for your needs.

Figure 37 Simple bricklaying methods

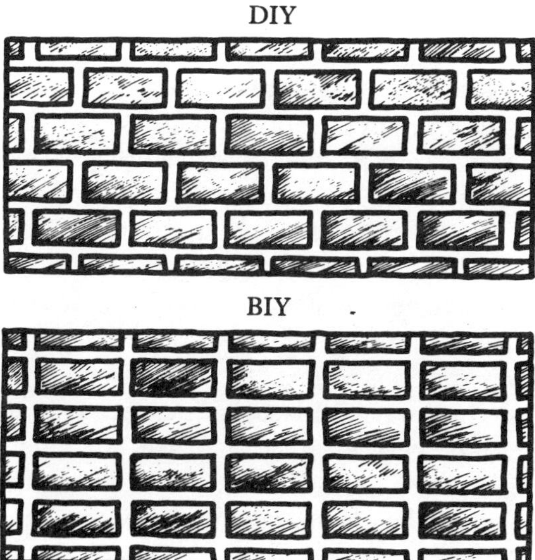

Historical note

Hadrian's Wall is a fine example of early outdoor constructions in this country. It also stands as proof that rivalry between Scottish and English soccer fans is no modern-day phenomenon.

The wall was built in early BC (before Croker) to prevent marauding Scottish fans from making their way to the Home International at Wembley Coliseum in Londinium.

The canny Scots soon got over this particular obstacle. Although security on the wall was tight, the Scottish fans got through by wrapping their long tartan scarves around their legs and pretending to be women. (This incidentally is thought to be the origin of the kilt.)

Of course many a Roman soldier, missing the orgies back home, would try to chat up these shy, heavily-built Scottish 'lasses', only to be rebuffed with a powerful blow to the head.

This left many a dazed centurion wondering how on earth a Scotsman ever got his oats.

Kitchen units

The large square 'tub' sink, big enough to bath the kids in; the walk-in larder with its glorious array of exotic aromas; and the less exotic but equally memorable odour of washing drying over the cooker on a Monday morning – these are all integral to life in the kitchens of yesteryear.

Since then, however, the kitchen, once in the complete and sole charge of the woman of the house, has been slowly sucking in the male of the species. From the day that man first heard the words 'Hygena fitted units' his fate was sealed. Where once he would have been expected to do no more than screw in a couple of cup hooks under the cupboard, he is now expected to turn his hand to any number of complex and tedious tasks.

A kitchen nowadays has to be unitised and designed for efficiency. There is a place for everything, and everything has its place, so long as it's not more than 600mm high, 600mm wide or 600mm deep. The floor cannot simply be covered with a square of linoleum; the glasses cannot simply be lined up on a shelf; the cutlery cannot simply lie in a drawer.

The Neff guide

The arrival of a new kitchen in the household can be divided into two areas of responsibility: his and hers. Or, to rephrase it: 1. The selection and purchase (the easy bit); and 2. The installation (the hard bit). It's not too hard to work out which of the responsibilities will be allocated to you.

The initial arrival of thirty-five boxed units, cooker hoods, work surfaces, sinks, waste disposal units and vegetable racks will undoubtedly dazzle you momentarily. Once it sinks in that it is all self-assembly, however, that feeling of euphoria will pass.

So, armed with your Philips screwdriver, spirit level, several six-inch nails, and a controlled temper, you set to work.

The first thing to remember when fitting cabinets is that nothing need be level. All this talk of making sure that the units are on the same plane was dreamed up by unscrupulous people trying to make the installing of kitchen units sound as difficult as splitting the atom.

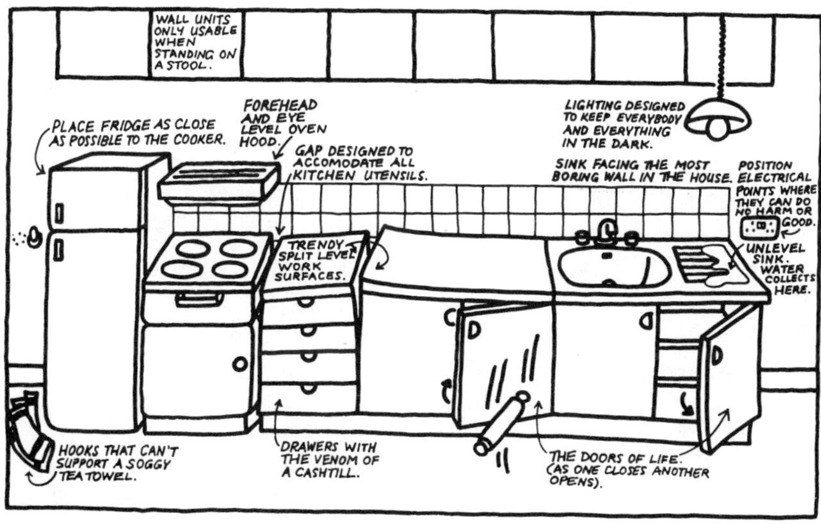

Figure 38

They thought that by playing on your natural fear of mathematics, and calculus in particular, they could extract vast quantities of printed paper from that thing closest to your heart: your wallet.

Install your units as they come. Once completed test to make sure that rolling pins roll and vegetables take on a life of their own.

The easiest way to get the general gist of what I'm saying is to observe Figure 38, where the basic rudiments of novel cuisine can be studied.

Bon appetit.

Plastering

Plastering has been likened to trying to nail porridge to the wall. And while trying to take care of the ceiling many a novice in this particular discipline has successfully plastered his floor.

For this reason even dutiful DIYers have avoided plastering like the plague in the past. Today all that has changed. Many specialised products have been introduced to make this task a lot easier and cleaner. These have, of course, been shunned by the true bodger who prefers the old ways and the feel of wet plaster in his turn-ups.

Insulating

The earliest form of home insulation was wrongly reported as the Window Tax of 1798. Lacking the advice of Ted Moult, enterprising bodgers would cut down the heat loss from their homes by cutting down on the number of windows. This they did by simply bricking them up.

Unfortunately, while making the home a little warmer this also cut down quite a bit on the light. These days there are a number of ingenious ways we can insulate the homestead without being left totally in the dark.

Loft insulation

No need to buy great rolls of expensive pink or yellow fibreglass insulation when you've got a ready-made answer in your wardrobe. Yes, you've finally found a practical use for all those oversized jumpers the mother-in-law knits you for Christmas.

Also, the loft is a perfect place to protect your priceless collection of girlie magazines from prying eyes.

Window insulation

There's a quick and easy way to stop the wind whistling through the gaps in your windows: masking tape. Use it to cover any gaps around the window. Similarly, excessive use of putty can also be helpful in stopping heat loss and saving on Windolene.

Figure 39

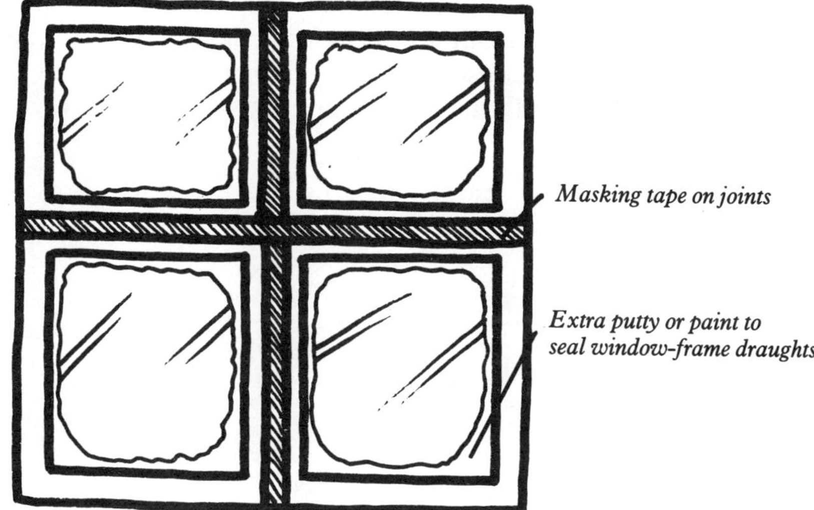

Door insulation

Any doorhanging that a bodger has any hand in will invariably mean a gap between the door and the floor that you could drive a bus through. To abate the howling wind the bodger will call upon his best friend – one of those little rag-doll dachshunds that never need feeding or taking for 'walkies'.

Glazing

Broken windows are a real pain. And while you may reason that they produce a cheap form of ventilation you will have to repair them sooner or later.

In the short term your beloved may let you get away (to the pub) with the old cover-up of Sellotape and brown paper (do not attempt this technique on

French windows, mon brave), but in the long term you will have to make a trip to the glazier. In doing so make sure that you return with a pane of glass that is slightly smaller than the space it needs to fill.

Compensate for this by using more than enough putty to hold the bulging glass in place. This will serve the double purpose of preventing heat loss through what little window the light doth penetrate.

Alternatively use the putty very sparingly, so that the next time you accidentally put the neighbour's new ladder up against the glass it will fall out in one piece, saving you the cost and trouble of buying another one.

Note: if employing the latter technique make sure you're always out when the window cleaner calls.

If it doesn't move, paint it

'DO YOU THINK I COULD BORROW . . .'

Anyone who has ever hammered a screw, hacksawed a piece of wood, or opened a can of paint with a chisel, knows that all this DIY lark can turn out to be rather expensive.

A chap starting out on the road to failure and wanting to equip himself for the journey ahead could walk out of most DIY stores having been done very nicely.

With the price of rawlplugs going through the roof, every bodger has to have his wits (as opposed to his cheque book) about him at all times if he is to avoid the fate of many a DIYer. In other words, being permanently boracic lint, without a bean and poorer than a church mouse.

By careful scrutiny of the DIY habits of your neighbours, you should be able to discover where to lay your hands on everything from a set of brushes to a high-speed hammer drill without spending a single penny.

But knowing where to lay one's hands on these basic tools and getting your hands on them are two entirely different matters. Once spotted, the item in question needs weeding out. The owner's confidence has to be gained and a sprinkling of lies must be employed. The easiest way to do this is to appeal to the DIYer's Achilles heel: Pride. That same pride that forces him to show off his beautifully maintained tools whenever he gets the chance. That same pride that turns a five-minute visit into a two-hour tour of the new family room/laundry room/bar.

Your average DIYer brushes his lawn mower down after every outing, rolls up the garden hose after a sprinkling, dusts off the saw after he's finished the Wendy House, and can find his cache of one-and-a-half-inch screws in the dark. He never misplaces a screwdriver, never spills nails into the cracks between the floorboards (although one could argue that this is because there are no cracks between his floorboards), and never puts the drill back without neatly winding up its cord. One compliment about his collection of backnuts and he's yours. Appeal to his vanity and you'll be walking out of his garage with more goodies than a Blankety Blank winner.

Breaking the ice

The first approach, once the target has been spotted, is best kept simple. Try popping round on a Saturday night just after the shops have shut and in the full knowledge that he has the tool you want. 'I'm in the middle of putting up some shelves in the kitchen,' you say, 'but I seem to have mislaid my electric drill chuck key. You wouldn't have one I could borrow, would you?'

No decent-minded, self-respecting DIYer would let another member of the cloth hang in mid-job on a Saturday night. You are on your way.

Now there are two courses he can follow: 1. Ask you to wait while he fetches the key you want; 2. Invite you to come through to his garage to help him find the spare you require.

The second is the first step on the downward path of pride. The door opens and suddenly there before you lies an embarrassment of riches usually confined to the centrefold of *Practical Householder*. There is a place for everything and everything in its place. On the walls the drills, the spanners, the saws and the paint brushes hang on their allotted hooks, all correct and raring to go. On the shelves all the nuts, bolts, nails and screws are neatly stored away and marked in old Nescafé jars with lids nailed to the undersides of shelves. Around the walls are workmates, extension cables, garden hoses and ladders all hung like priceless paintings in an art gallery. On the work bench are the sanders, vices and cutting machines, while a special rack contains the useful offcuts of wood.

Once inside this Aladdin's Cave, there is no escape for the DIYer, no going back. For the bodger has seen with his own eyes. Has touched with his own hands.

For the unsuspecting DIYer, the months of torment are about to commence.

After the ice is broken – more common techniques

During my recent public house-to-house survey of BIY indulgers, I found that the most popular secondary form of 'Do you think I could borrow . . .' is the 'Garden Wall' approach as shown in Figure 40.

Friends, bodgers, countrymen, lend me your shears

Figure 40 The over-the-garden-hedge technique

Fast, simple and efficient, this technique is usually employed in the earlier stages of the campaign, when you're still on speaking terms and the lender is still happy to hand over one or more of his favourite things.

To ring the changes and freshen a slightly tarnished relationship (by now some of the DIYer's tools will look the same way) the 'Holiday' technique is very effective for renewed borrowing.

Just keep your eyes and ears peeled for signs of an approaching holiday and get in there for a sander, lawn mower and a monkey wrench or two. Better still, with a little bit of persuasion you can obtain the key to the garage for the holiday period on the pretext that you will be keeping an eye on things for him. Unsure of the wisdom of this action our DIY holidaymaker will have to be restrained from turning back at Dover. Certainly, after two weeks in the sun, his tanned face is bound to be drained chalky white at the sight of the workshop he knew and loved.

Figure 41 demonstrates the quick-thinking ability that every keen bodger must possess. Remember, it's easier to borrow something that the lender isn't using all the time.

During your many trips to his workshop, sharp eyes and simple mathematics will ascertain if any of his equipment is doubled up. From this position a good bodger can negotiate a more permanent loan of tools, otherwise known as 'the point of no return'. See Figure 42.

Figure 41 *The 'As-I-see-you're-not-using . . .' technique*

Figure 42 *The 'I-see-you've-got-two-of-these' technique*

At some time in the not too far distant future (possibly as soon as a month) you'll find it a problem asking for, and getting, more equipment. Don't fret; there's still one more ploy you can use which will probably work for a week or two. A direct approach during the day from your wife to his wife could mean a few more useful items come into your possession before he's any the wiser. If you are adopting this technique, however, it is advisable not to let your loved one in on the details of your plan. She'd only make you give everything back.

Figure 43 The 'Jeff-asked-if-he-could-borrow-Alan's . . .' technique

Possession is nine-tenths of the law

Once you've got the equipment safely in your hands, you might as well treat it as though it were your own. Just because it really belongs to a man who always reads the manufacturer's instructions is no reason for you to change your ways. Nor should you feel any guilt when you catch him staring over the hedge at his hand saw lying on your lawn. A DIYer will always go out and replace any missing or needed tools – that's part of the complex. If you look at it that way, you are not so much depriving him or causing him inconvenience as giving him the opportunity to always have the latest model.

Figure 44
Use his chisels as though they were your own

BIY

SO FAR . . . SO BAD

Here's a little questionnaire to find out how much you've taken in of this, the first encyclopaedia of bodging.

Now's the time to discover whether you're able to move away from DIY at all, and answer the sixty-four-million-dollar question: whether or not you're ready to come out of that closet and embrace BIY totally.

The questionnaire won't reveal all that's lurking in the innermost parts of your brain, but it will give a good indication of your general attitude to DIY, BIY, the priesthood, Gay Liberation, Sunday shopping, Jan Leeming's hair-styles, next door's Alsatian and all the other priorities of life.

Good luck.

Never do today what you can bodge tomorrow

Question 1

The ensuite shower attached to the ensuite bathroom adjacent to the master bedroom has sprung a rather inconvenient leak. Do you . . .

a. Attach one end of a flexible hose to the gusher and put the other end under the mattress, thus solving the problem and creating your own water bed at the same time.

b. Claim that this will dispel any worries the wife might have had about dry rot once and for all.

c. Get the wife to do the old 'little Dutch boy with his finger in the dyke' trick. This may be where the expression 'My Old Dutch' comes from.

d. Stop it with some electrical tape and a plastic bag.

Question 2

It is a wonderful Saturday morning. Your nose gently rises above the edge of your Mary Quant quilt to greet another perfect day. There's the satisfying clink of milk bottles on the doorstep, and you are just relishing the prospect of Tony Lewis's cricket reports when the wife asks you to fix the lock on the bathroom door. Do you . . .

a. Remind her that you removed the bathroom door two days ago.

b. Not being able to think of anything, resort to passion.

c. Do it for the sake of peace and quiet. Even bodgers have days off.

d. Fix the lock so nobody can get in and nobody can get out.

Question 3

The hire shop rather unreasonably wants its cement mixer back. Well, you have had it for six months. However, there is a slight problem about its return. The machine in question seems to have done a bunk from your driveway. Do you . . .

a. Tell the hire shop that it has been kidnapped by a fanatical group of fast food addicts who are at this very moment mixing the biggest pizza in the world complete with black olives and mozzarella cheese.

b. Claim that the machine was stolen by a shortsighted entrant to the London–Brighton vintage car rally and that it would be unwise to stand in his way.

c. Explain that it has been borrowed by the Golden Duck Chinese restaurant who are using it to place their customer's palm prints in the wet cement of the pavement outside their humble establishment and you haven't the heart to tell them that a Mr Grauman already thought of the idea.

Question 4

A series of heating bills has arrived through your letterbox, providing yet more fuel for the 'Insulate Your Home' lobby. Brochures featuring easy to install double glazing, loft insulation and DIY cavity wall insulation are thrust accusingly under your nose. Do you . . .

a. Start wearing 'Heat the World' badges.

b. Enrol the whole family in night school for knitting.

c. Turn off all the heaters and walk around in your bermuda shorts complaining about the longest Indian summer ever.

d. Cover all the windows with cling wrap.

Question 5

Most of the paint you put on the outside of the house three years ago has now fallen off and the word has it that you're going to be asked to do it all over again. Do you . . .

a. Start extolling the virtues of stone cladding (aided by a few brochures) and suggest that purple paintwork would make a nice contrast.

b. Bring out the Hitchcock 'Vertigo' syndrome. Start getting the old dizzy attacks every time you chance to stand on anything higher than two inches off the ground.

c. Lend all your ladders to the chap down the road and tell him not to hurry to get them back for a few months.

d. Start working on the ground-floor paintwork at such a rate that the wife's cherished hydrangeas are completely covered in white sandtex, in the hope that she will soon be pleading with you to stop further undesirable cover-ups.

Question 6

The Acacia Avenue Tenants Association, the NSPCC, the Council and the local Round Table have been at you for months to clear the mess and building rubble from your front garden. Do you . . .

a. Complain vehemently about the plague of moles that has infested your garden, destroying your crazy paving, ornamental goldfish pond and rockery.

b. Offer the entire front garden to the Tate Gallery suggesting that at £50 all in it was £1950 cheaper than the last pile of bricks they bought.

c. Explain that you're building an adventure playground for the underprivileged children of the area.

d. Say that there's a backlog of skips at the moment but you have been assured that one will turn up any day now.

Question 7

You move into a new house, and the next door neighbour mistakes you for a DIYer and asks your advice about constructing a garden wall. Do you . . .

a. Take him down to the Two Ferrets for a few pints and a gentle indoctrination course in the finer aspects of BIY.

b. Going by memory and what you've learnt from the boxed instructions with your son's Lego kit (and because it's his wall and not yours) give him all the advice he wants.

c. Hit him with red tape explaining that he'll need planning permission from the council, a permit from the Noise Abatement Society, a licence from the local dog's home, etc., etc.

d. Explain the futility of building a wall when there's going to be a bypass built smack in the middle of his garden in two years' time.

Question 8

None of the windows in the living room now open because you've painted over all the joints. The wife wants to bring some fresh air into the room during the annual spring clean. Do you . . .

a. Take a hammer and chisel to the offending windows blaming the resulting chipped paintwork on the incredibly harsh frost there was last night.

b. Tell her that you've put in a very expensive draught excluder and to open the windows would destroy the seal.

c. Talk wildly about acid rain

d. Accidentally release the pet budgie from its cage.

Question 9

Hi-tech kitchens are now all the rage on the avenue. Microwaves, ceramic hobs and computer-controlled washing machines have now been put on the shopping list for your house. You, of course, prefer to remain a firm believer in the world according to a coal scuttle. Do you . . .

a. Enrol for a course on semi-conductor micro-electronics at the Poly every

Thursday night, explaining, 'It's only a five-year course, pet, and I think it's best I understand the new technology before we start shelling out good money.'

b. Remind her of the trouble she had mastering the hoover.

c. Start employing the same lateral thinking you did when the wife asked for a more efficient lawn mower and you bought a goat.

d. Paint your present kitchen cabinets glossy black, stick a red quartz clock on the wall and put an electric motor in the mangle.

Question 10

The dining room has now been half-painted, half-wallpapered and half-carpeted for the last six months. Although this isn't unreasonable by bodging standards, the wife is now verging on violence. Do you . . .

a. Suggest six people she hates to be invited to the first dinner party in the finished dining room.

b. Remind her of her marriage vows and the bit about sharing worldly goods and give her the tools to keep her half of the contractual agreement.

c. Shy off, saying you can't remember which of the halves you've finished and which ones you hadn't.

d. Knuckle down and put a couple of rolls of paper on the wall, a little paint on the ceiling and a bit of underfelt on the bare floorboards in the hope that it will buy you a little more time.

Question 11

The wallpaper you put up yesterday has bubbled up, peeled and shrunk. There's a lot of flak flying your way. Do you . . .

a. Point to the three rolls out of the ten you put up that have stood their ground and reason that a 70% failure rate isn't at all bad.

b. Blame the recent rerouting of Jumbo jets over your house.

c. Identify the cause of the problem as the wife's fault for leaving the central heating on all night.

d. Blame it on the manufacturer.

Question 12

The next door neighbour has noticed traces of woodworm in his house. Rentokill are convinced that it's coming from your house. Do you . . .

a. Claim that it isn't woodworm at all but the result of the previous occupant having trouble finding a floor joist when nailing down the floorboards.

b. Quickly carpet the living room.

c. Explain, patiently, that woodworm are good for the wood because the little holes improve the airflow under the floorboards and prevent it from becoming warped.

d. Explain that these are teeth marks made by a little known animal, the beaver rat, which is prevalent in the area and, unfortunately, a protected species.

Question 13

You are tired of tripping over the kids' books and games every time you go in to kiss them good night. It is time you broke down and put up the shelves you've been promising for the last nine months. You've got the shelving, you've got almost the right sized brackets, you've got the screws, you've got rawlplugs, and you even have the approximate drill bit. Only thing is, there is a fantastic 1930s mystery on the television that you have always wanted to see. The shelves, if you do them the way Stan would do them, will take two hours to put up. The movie starts in forty-five minutes. Do you . . .

a. Put up one shelf, at least it's a beginning?

b. Forget the movie, it'll come back on in another eight years?

c. Swear to high heaven that you will do the shelves tomorrow morning, forget the Sunday lie-in?

d. Use a six-inch nail and warn the kids that they shouldn't slam the bedroom door, put anything too heavy on the shelves, or accidentally knock against them?

Your score

Add up your final total with the points awarded for each answer as given here.

a. 1, b. 1, c. 1, d. 1.

How did you do then?

If you didn't score 13 points after answering all the questions give yourself an extra point. Of course, I cheated a little. The answer to all of the questions was, in fact, a six-inch nail. However, as you are a relatively inexperienced bodger you were not to know this. In any event, doing this quiz has wasted a good five minutes that could otherwise have been spent fixing something. Well done, professor.

DIYers do it by the book

THE HISTORY OF BODGING

We all know at least one person who found the mains when nailing in the towel rail.

Or someone who plunged the house into darkness after putting a new plug on the toaster.

Or the improvement enthusiast who took out the fireplace a little too enthusiastically and ended up in his neighbour's living room.

If you sat down and thought about it, you could probably come up with a whole list of incipient bodgers in your street alone.

What I'd like to do now is introduce you to some of the bodgers that, in the words of Michael Caine, 'not a lot of people know about'.

First of all, bodging has been around for a lot longer than DIY. A lot longer.

In fact, the roots of bodging can be traced back as far as 3000 BC (Before Cement) when a group of unknown builders unsuccessfully attempted to construct the world's first high rise office block on Salisbury Plain. Ever since then, bodgers great and small have left their mark on the landscape.

Like Woodward and Bernstein of Watergate fame, my researchers have unearthed the truth about some of the more famous bodges that DIYers have tried to cover up. It wasn't an easy task. They had to endure many long hours in the unwelcome atmosphere of strange public houses, forced to drink alcoholic beverages in order to escape detection. And many more historic bodge-ups still remain undetected. Given time and the relaxing of the opening hours, all will eventually be revealed.

In the meanwhile, read on McDuff.

THE MERCEDES 300 SL

In 1954, an enterprising production manager at Mercedes-Benz in Germany became an unwitting member of our exclusive brotherhood.

Like all great bodgers', his idea was simplicity itself: why not let a robot carry out all the laborious jobs on the production line? No need for Schnapps breaks, obertime or holidays on the Costa del Sol.

So our production manager introduced the Board to ERNST, the less frivolous robot brother of England's computer ERNIE.

ERNST was programmed to carry out the mechanical functions required to produce a motorcar (remember, this was long before the Italians ever started playing opera muzak to their robots). Anyway, in all the rush to get things moving on the assembly line, our unsung hero forgot to tell ERNST about car doors.

One weekend, the Board decided to put ERNST into full production and closed down the factory to all humans while they went off on a Rhine boat party with James Last. When they returned on the Montag they discovered, to their horror, 10,000 Mercedes-Benz sportscars with an unusual feature.

Instead of the car door hinges being set at the side of the door, they were at the top. One nervous director shouted 'Mein Gott, vot ar vee going to do viz all dees Albatrosses?' But one of the other directors had an idea. Why not call the car the 'gull wing' and pretend that the up-swinging door idea was intentional?

'Wunderbar' was the unanimous reply.

Of course, ERNST had to go. The Germans, disguising a titter or two, sold the robot to an Italian motor manufacturer who wanted to monitor rust prevention.

ERNST didn't like this job very much and several thousand rusting hulks later was sacked. Pronto.

The last anyone heard of ERNST it was engaged in the production of a rustproof, gull wing sportscar in Northern Ireland.

Surely nothing could go wrong now, could it?

THE WORLD'S TRADE CENTER(S)

This humdinger of a bodge-up remains unclaimed by its perpetrator for reasons that will quickly become apparent.

Although the good old Big Apple already stood knee deep in skyscrapers, back in the late 1960s the New York City Planner's Office decided they needed just one more. Called the World's Trade Center (a modest little title by American standards) this shining monument to the Land of Opportunity would stand in the southern part of Manhattan island.

The planners invited eminent architects to submit designs for the construction, and blueprints and models came in faster than orders for popcorn at an American movie house.

Builders were also asked to give their quotes based upon the chosen design, a simple construction of glass and concrete.

After much deliberation (on expenses and on the town), the planners made their final choice of builders from a shortlist of two. And here's where our mysterious bodger played his or her ace card, for it seems that the letter of confirmation was incorrectly sent to both candidates.

After a mild celebration at the Palm restaurant and Sardi's respectively, both construction companies turned up on the site somewhat bleary-eyed. Without knowledge of the bodge-up back at the City Planner's Office, each company ignored the other's presence, assuming that it was working on a totally different project. The site was certainly big enough.

Soon both had laid the foundations for their identical buildings. And not much later, both were a few storeys high.

Not long after that, a competitive element crept into the building as each company tried to out-storey the other. By now both had realised that something was up, and it wasn't just the buildings.

The original plans called for 55 storeys. At 65 storeys, both companies were still racing skyward. And so it was at 75, and 85, and 95.

A little late in the day, the City planners paid a visit to the site and found themselves in double trouble.

Now in three-figure storeys, our over-zealous builders had finally run out of materials. And while they had their heads in the clouds, the planners held theirs in their hands.

Because there it was, the World's Trade Center.

And just like a bad dream, over there it was again, the World's Trade Center.

They looked like two gigantic stereo speakers and the City planners were wondering how they were going to explain this one to the hard-nosed populace of New York.

In the end it was a theatre-going member of their group who reminded them of the song 'New York, New York' and suggested that everything was not only bigger and better in the old city of New Amsterdam, but twice as good. Hence the necessity for two World's Trade Centers.

Give that man a two week vacation with Bo Derek in an Atlanta motel, they all yelled.

Now City planners are looking into doing similar things with other important landmarks in their great Doppelgänger city. How about *two* Statues of Liberty. Giving your regards to *two* Broadways. Or indeed having breakfast at *two* Tiffanys.

However, because of a singular inability to win anything but the wooden spoon, New Yorkers have decided not to duplicate their football team.

Well, even Americans have feelings.

VENICE

Back in the eighth century a group of wandering Italian merchants were fed up with being harassed by boorish Barbarians and the like. A real estate agent in Rome was briefed to find them a place were the neighbours were a little friendlier, and trips were arranged for the merchants to view splendid plots in what we now call Naples and Florence. But they were all a little too molto expensivo for the now desperate merchants. As a last resort they agreed to view what the estate agent described as 'an endearing little plot in a lagoon in the Veneto region of Northern Italy'.

The merchants loved the spot. Everywhere was within walking distance of the sea, and they all agreed that it had a wonderful creative atmosphere. Whether intoxicated by the sheer joy of finally finding somewhere to hang up the old codpiece in quiet, or by a little too much Bardolino, they signed a long lease without having a surveyor give it the quick once-over. Their first attempts at construction all sank majestically back into the sand. The soil was no better than an over-ripe Bel Paese.

One day a young stonemason, Signor Gino Frascati, entered the soggy piazza and suggested a scheme to drive stone piles into the spongy ground and thus provide the foundation needed to support an entire city. This sounded like a pretty good idea at the time. After all, why do something simple like move a couple of miles down the road to Rimini when you can build a whole city on stilts?

Work began immediately. The new and very happy residents built churches, palaces, wide streets and stunning piazzas with unprecedented splendour and love. When the city was finished everyone was extremely pleased with the way it had turned out. But the celebrations were shortlived.

After a few high tides the city began to sink along with its foundations back into the Adriatic. The wide roads became permanently submerged, so the quick-thinking Venetians decided to re-name them canals. Nevertheless, those who had invested their hard earned lire in basement flats were none too pleased with developments. The only happy residents appeared to be members of the recently formed Venice Sub Aqua club.

Our master stonemason, needless to say, was not the most popular man on the piazza. Not easily defeated, however, Gino soon came up with a brilliant bit of bodging logic and foresight, explaining that perhaps things weren't quite as bad as everybody thought. He talked about the attractions of a semi-submerged city: how people would flock from all over the world to see such a sight; how it would be the perfect place for canoodling couples to spend romantic weekends.

And, indeed, he was right. Tourists began arriving in their thousands. Taxi drivers took gondola lessons, ensuring that Venice was the only place you could get a taxi when it was wet. Most hotels boasted their own indoor swimming pools.

Venice became a success overnight – and all thanks to the quick thinking of one master bodger.

THE PARIS ARTS CENTRE

We need look no further than the artistic city of Paris for our next example of bodging; in particular, the new Arts Centre.

Carrying on in the finest traditions of our Italian friend, this was the handiwork of a British architect, Richard Rogers.

He was commissioned to design the ultra-modern new arts complex in the heart of the city. Like any good bodger, our man favoured speed rather than attention to detail in the execution of his task. So, without further ado, plans were drawn up and building completed before you could say 'Maurice Chevalier'.

It was only then that our friend discovered something was missing from his cultural masterpiece. Specifically, the heating and air ventilation systems.

The Parisians were none too pleased with the way things had developed and they put pressure on our architect friend to put things right before somebody lost their head to Madame La Guillotine. However, public response to our hero's first solution to this little oversight – 900 strategically-placed two-bar convector heaters and a similar number of three-speed desktop electric fans – was not favourable. It was then, with the calm and dash of a seasoned bodger, that Citizen Rogers found the perfect answer to the problem: he stuck all the piping and ducts on the outside of the Arts Centre.

The Parisians were stunned by our man's simple logic. To heighten the effect, our bodger had the pipes and ducts painted different colours. This was to be a great help to maintenance men when it came to identifying certain pipes as they were lowered down by helicopter – the only way they could now get at the system stuck forty feet up in the air on the side of the building.

Nice one, n'est-ce pas?

THE HOVERCRAFT

Perhaps the most unusual bodge of all time happened in 1955.

That year the Ministry of Supply asked inventor and general clever dick Christopher Cockerell to design a vacuum cleaner big enough to sweep down the corridors of power and remove the many tons of clerical grey dust that daily settled there.

Cockerell went to work on the project in his seaside premises quite unaware that he was about to rise above such mundane things as cleaning appliances. Soon he had built a vacuum cleaner of quite staggering proportions. So big was it, that an outboard power unit had to be fitted and a rubber skirt used to protect Government Issue furniture when it ultimately whizzed up and down.

Mr Cockerell decided to give the machine its first test run on a sunny day in 1959, and he invited the men from the Ministry down to watch. He had no doubts that his machine would work perfectly.

Anticipation was high as everyone gathered around the machine in Cockerell's workshop.

Cockerell, ready to steer the great machine over the deliberately laid trail of dust, powder and assorted droppings, gave his assistant the signal to throw the switch. But the anxious fellow, unsure about exactly which switch to throw, threw the lot. And in doing so put the vast machine, not into suck, but on to blow.

The result is history.

With a giant shudder the machine sprang into life, lifted clear off the hangar floor and proceeded to start bounding off the four walls of the workshop like an enormous pinball. Terrified ministers fled through the hangar's wide doors, hotly pursued by Mr Cockerell and his erratic invention. They were greatly relieved when the machine suddenly veered to the left, in the general direction of the open sea.

They thought this was the end of Mr Cockerell and his infernal machine, but they were wrong. Once upon the glassy smooth sea the machine was in its true element. Soon Cockerell had got the hang of the steering and was able to demonstrate the machine's manoeuvrability.

The men from the Ministry, ever able to change direction at a moment's notice, immediately hit upon the idea of using the machine as a ferry. One young blood even dreamt up a name for the new conveyance: the Hoovercraft.

Unfortunately, owing to a slip in a Whitehall typing pool, the name of the machine was reduced to the Hovercraft.

The name stuck. And Mr Cockerell, rather unsteadily, entered the Bodgers' Hall of Fame.

THE BUNGALOW

Now, not all great bodges have been on the grandest scale. As every bodger knows, it's not how much you bodge that counts, but how well you bodge it.

Take the touching tale of the inventive housebuilder whom we shall call Keenan Eager. His real name must remain a secret for reasons of security. (His.)

Our errant builder was asked to construct a perfectly ordinary two-storey house somewhere out in suburbia. Nothing too difficult, you would have thought. The plans were duly drawn up, local council permission granted, and the all clear given to start ordering materials. To prepare himself for the arduous task ahead, our man indulged in a time-honoured bodging ritual and took his trusty workforce down to the local hostelry for a refresher course in the finer points of bricklaying.

Keenan placed the plans in his back pocket for safe keeping while he set about demolishing a few pints. Only when he and his team were suitably ready and the publican particularly insistent on closing did our man start work.

And so it was that, eyeing his plans with an unsteady gaze, he made a slight miscalculation – something that could happen to anyone with a crease in his plans.

After the foundations had been laid the house soon started to take shape and everything was going well until the diligent brickies asked where the rest of the bricks were.

'Rest of the bricks?' Keenan echoed quizzically as the men pointed to the spot where the bricks had been neatly piled.

It was then that our man realised that the crease in his plans had put a considerable dent in his estimation.

With the proud owner of the house about to make a call at any moment to see how everything was going, our bodger had to think fast. Undeterred by the sight of only half a two-storey house before him, he commanded his bemused workforce to 'bung a low roof on it'.

Well, why not.

And with that one simple and inspired act our bodger wrote a new chapter in the history of housebuilding, and the bungalow was born.

At a stroke he had not only halved the cost of building a house, but had also given the new bungalow owners other savings to look forward to. Savings like lower heating bills. No outlay on stair carpets. And the inexpensive installation of TV aerials.

Of course, for those people with a fear of highliving, vertigo to be precise, the bungalow was an added boon. With everything on the ground floor, the only thing to make a bungalow owner dizzy was the boldness of the chicken vindaloo from the Indian takeaway.

As for our bodging friend Keenan, he now offers his dubious talents as a landscape gardener. 'Remember, Keenan, green side up, green side up'.

PISA

One of the earliest exponents of BIY was an Italian architect commissioned to build a tower in a nondescript little town some time in the twelfth century. The tradesmen of the area had prospered and now looked to improve the appearance of their town and enhance its importance in the general scheme of things. With this aim in mind they wanted a magnificent tower to complement their new church and town square.

And that's where young Bonnano Pisan comes in.

Needless to say, showing commendable BIY craft, the young Italian totally ignored the geologist's reports and went ahead with his tower, employing a finishing speed that would leave the goalkeeper of Juventus flatfooted. He also restricted the depth of the foundations to ten feet, thereby saving valuable drinking time.

The work was just beginning to take shape when the project took on a whole new slant. (Literally.) It became a listed building before its time.

Although he had managed to complete three floors, the tower never looked like straightening itself out. Irate councillors called upon poor Bonnano for an explanation. They warned that it had better be a good one.

They had already taken the precaution of calling Rent-A-Mobster and Bonnano looked all set to prop up one of the flyovers on the new stretch of autostrada if he didn't give the right answer.

Well, before our friend was carried away by two large men in navy blue overcoats he explained that conventional straight towers were two a lira in Italy, and that one day his tower would put their insignificant town on the map.

The plan didn't work, unfortunately. To this very day Bonnano remains a pillar of support to motorists on the way between Milan and Bologna.

The tower itself was eventually completed, though it never looked like becoming an upright member of the community.

Bonnano's words did come true, of course. Today everybody has heard of the famous Leaning Tower of Pisa. But how many straight Italian towers can you put a name to?

FROM THE DESK OF JEFF SLAPDASH

Dear Jeff,

My wife and I have just bought a run-down house which we intend 'doing up'. I have no previous experience of BIY and am worried about not doing it right.

How do I start, and more important, where?

Worried,
Chipping-Off-The-Old-Block,
Gloucs.

Dear Worried,

There's really nothing to fret about, Nobby.

Bodging for the first time can be a joyous thing. Just remember that there are no rules and no standards but your own.

Flit from one project to another, leaving no stone unturned, as your whimsy dictates. It is unnecessary to finish anything.

Start fresh. Take a sledgehammer to the walls. Unhinge a few doors. Undermine a few foundations. At the end of the month you'll be able to stand back and admire your handiwork and architectural imagination.

For any further advice don't hesitate to call.

My door is always open (mainly because I put it on myself and now can't shut it).

yours in a draught,

Jeff Slapdash

Dear Jeff,

After thirteen years of accomplished bodging a recent problem has caused me a lot of embarrassment with my fellow bodgers at the local.

You see, for the last six months I've continued to get things right. DIY is what I mean. The wife's ecstatic, naturally, but I'm beginning to think that I may never bodge again.

For example, I put some shelves up in the kitchen last week that are as solid as the Rock of Gibraltar. I replaced a roof tile and it actually stopped the leak. I laid a carpet in the hallway at the weekend and nobody's tripped over it yet.

Tell me, Jeff, what can I do to get things back to normal?

yours,
Don,
Bloomsbury

Dear Don,

Fairly common complain this one, Nobby.

What you have to do is forget the past and remember the gold bodging rules. Then when you feel an attack of dreaded DIY coming on refer to the bodger's teachings.

Now when it came to fixing those shelves, I bet we forgot the golden 'who needs rawlplugs' rule, didn't we?

As for the roof tile, well, that could happen to anyone.

Better luck next time. Remember, chin up, and head down in the *Sporting Life*.

yours,

Doctor Slapdash

Dear Jeff,

Let me first congratulate you on the sterling job you are doing in getting BIY recognised.

I too have struggled to carry the flag of bodging. It hasn't been easy, Jeff, I can tell you. People used to point at me in the street and throw bricks back into the house (known locally as The Swamp).

I was a marked man (they were pretty good at brick-throwing). But I have shouldered the responsibility of keeping BIY alive in my area.

Soon I hope to hold evening classes for other would-be bodgers ready to come out of the closet.

Thanks once again for giving humble bodgers like me hope for the future.

yours gratefully,
Robin Lloyd-Banks,
Shooter's Hill,
London S.E.17

Dear Robin,

Or may I call you Nobby? Your letter has moved me.

You are one of the true bodging pioneers my book was dedicated to. Your tireless efforts have not been in vain, be assured of that, my old son.

One day they'll build a statue to you. It's unlikely to stand up for very long, but that's life for you.

Keep up the good fight, Nobby.

yours in the shade,

Jeff Slapdash

Dear Mr Slapdash,

It has come to my attention that you are advocating everything that decent, law-abiding *Guardian* readers and DIYers like myself are against.

I put it to you, sir, that you and your organisation are the biggest single threat to this Nation's heritage since that Austrian painter and decorator back in 1939.

I implore you to give up this foolishness and return to the fold. DIY isn't all that bad once you get used to the monotony.

yours, with concern,
Hugh Jarse,
Swinely Bottom

Dear Hugh,

Well, Nobby, yours is not the first letter of this kind I have received, and I'm sure it won't be the last.

But let's face facts, BIY is here to stay (until it falls down, that is). BIY gives the mind a chance to conquer insurmountable problems at a stroke.

And may I say that I detect a certain dissatisfaction with your own lot. Why not open your heart, and your neighbour's workshop, and embrace BIY. Think of the fun you could have at somebody else's expense.

Come out of the closet, Hugh, and see how much fun life is on the other side of a badly constructed garden fence.

yours persuasively,

Jeff Slapdash

Dear Jeff,

Word has just reached me that you have recently opened up a tool hire company.

I must say I find this rather odd, and somewhat contrary to your BIY beliefs.

Explain please.

Bemused, bothered and bewildered,
Ikenham,
Cambridgeshire

Dear Nobby,

Let me put your bodging mind at rest.

I do have a hire shop, yes. It is available to bodgers on the basis that we've never ever got what you want in stock.

This is, of course, nothing new to the hire shop trade, but where mine really scores is that when there is something in the shop it invariably never works.

For example, we've got cement mixers with motors so burnt out you couldn't mix a fairy cake. Electric drills with reverse motors which make drilling through plasterboard like scratching at granite. Scaffolding systems that are so mixed up you'd be lucky to find enough of the same type to scaffold a mousehole. We've got wallpaper steamers that could possibly be of use to a philatelist wishing to lift a stamp or two.

So you see, my hire shop is designed to give bodgers hours, weeks and sometimes months of delayed activity.

Remember, a bad workman should always blame his tools. I'm just throwing a spanner in to help.

Oh ye of little faith.

Jeff Slapdash,
Hire and Hire Ltd

Dear Jeffrey,

While so far being more than happy with the BIY projects I've been attempting on a day-to-day basis – or should I say year-to-year basis – I feel an urge to take on something a little more adventurous.

What advice would you give me about projects like extensions, loft conversions, swimming pools, etc.?

Am I ready for these?

A. M. Bitious,
Barking

Dear A. M.,

Your letter fills me with pride and hope for the future of bodging (not to mention my publisher's advance for my next opus, in the bookshops soon: *BIY for Advanced Bodgers*).

The movement is obviously going places.

God knows where, but here's hoping.

As for your question, well, I'm actually in the process of setting up weekend seminars in Advanced Bodging where all the skills you require for the projects you've mentioned will be totally ignored.

The seminars have been offered a Costa Brava hotel as the venue. However, there is always a risk that the building won't be ready in time, thanks to some imaginative work by our Spanish cousin, El Bodger.

I'll keep you posted.

Jeffrey Slapdash

BODGER BEWARE

Now that you've read this book you will appreciate that a bodger skates on pretty thin ice.

This after all is the attraction of bodging.

A DIYer gets no marks for originality or daring.

However, even a bodger can overdo it and we'd like to draw your attention to one such case reported here.

Now, over the next few months your wife (or husband indeed) will see a marked change in your outlook to jobs around the house.

At first they may be forgiven for thinking that you have gone completely off your trolley.

But later on they will catch the drift of your little wheeze.

And that's when you must temper your bodging activities with a little caution.

Don't try to do too much too soon.

You've got plenty of time, dear bodger.

Inefficient handyman divorced

A woman whose handyman husband started many jobs in the house and garden, but seldom finished them, was granted a divorce in the High Court in London yesterday.

Her kitchen had been in disarray for years, he left tools around the house, in Lower Kingswood, Surrey, and the garden was full of builders materials and old cars.

no
school
ting holi
39 weeks
on a 52-wee
The uni
contracts
women a
refused we
Lord J
that the
breach of a
which was
matter in the
relations.
He added
surprising
not enth
the uni
their
the n
of

Dearer juice

A litre of or uice will
by 6p from

THE BOOK THEY'RE ALL TALKING ABOUT . . .

'. . . a nightmare from start to finish . . .'
DO IT YOURSELF

'Is he serious?'
PRACTICAL HOUSEHOLDER

'It could put British interior design back 100 years'
GOOD HOUSEKEEPING

'We're looking forward to a big upturn in sales'
THE BREWERS SOCIETY

'He's taken it very hard'
DAVID HICKS' PERSONAL SECRETARY

'Jeff Slapdash should be shot'
BARRY BUCKNELL